Eating Like Queens

Eating Like Queens

A Guide to Ethnic Dining in America's Melting Pot, Queens, New York

Suzanne Parker

JONES
BOOKS
Madison, Wisconsin

Jones Books
309 N. Hillside Ter.
Madison, Wisconsin 53705-3328
www.jonesbooks.com

First printing, first edition

Book and cover design by Pentagram, Austin

Photographs by Suzanne Parker

Library of Congress Cataloging-in-Publication Data

Parker, Suzanne, 1947-
    Eating like queens : a guide to ethnic dining in America's melting
pot, Queens, New York / Suzanne Parker.— 1st ed.
        p. cm.
    Includes index.
    ISBN-13: 978-0-9763539-0-4 (alk. paper)
    1. Ethnic restaurants—New York (State)—New York—Guidebooks.
2. Cookery, International. 3. Queens (New York, N.Y.)—Guidebooks.
I. Title.
    TX907.3.N72N467 2005
    647.95747'243—dc22
                                                    2005009010

Printed in South Korea

For Andrew Parker, my husband and love of my life, eating buddy, severest critic, and biggest supporter.

TABLE OF CONTENTS

ACKNOWLEDGMENTS

PERHAPS BECAUSE IT IS THE FIRST language we learn, people love to talk about the food they eat. So many gave generously of their time, knowledge, samplings of their tidbits that for sure I will miss a few of you, so for that I apologize in advance.

I would like to thank the following for sharing food insights from their native countries: Adiyatwidi Adiwoso Asmady, Deputy Indonesian UN Ambassador; Leo Chiang; Sam Won Gahk; Paulette Clarke, MsWhirls Jerk Sauce; Tariq Hamid, Shaheen Foods; Ishle Park, Queens poet laureate; Rahita Raval, Bonelle Bakery; Paula Stevens, Paula Stevens Burecas.

I would also like to thank the following for their help and advice: Barbara McGregor, intrepid tasting companion, loyal friend, and giver of moral support; Kathy Eiring and May Schonhaut, Forest Hills Gardens Corporation; Ilana Harlow, folklorist, author of *The International Express*, and role model for my explorations; Peter Ochiogrosso, book publishing mentor; Terri Osborne, Spencer Ferdinand, Queens Economic Development Corp.; Kerim Friedman and Shashwati Talukdar.

Also, my agent Rosemary Stimola and publisher Joan Strasbaugh for giving me a chance.

And last, and perhaps most, Jim Leff and the posters from the Outer Boroughs Chowhound Board, who I have come to regard as my virtual friends. Chowhound.com was the source of many of my best leads, and a treasure trove of useful information.

INTRODUCTION

I'M A RARE BIRD. I WAS BORN in Queens and still live there. Rarely will you find someone living in Queens who is actually from Queens. When I was growing up in Rego Park, my neighbors were mostly from Brooklyn, on their way to moving to Long Island, or World War II refugees (think Art Spiegelman's *Maus*). Now my Queens neighbors are, without exaggeration, from everywhere, on their way to wherever. Think of a country, and there is probably a community of its expatriates somewhere in Queens. I'm grateful they brought food.

Queens is the most multicultural county in the United States, which probably makes it the most multicultural county in the world. The New York State comptroller estimates 138 languages are spoken there. Once upon a time, Queens was considered a bucolic suburb of a more congested Manhattan. Cultural icons like Rudolf Valentino and Irving Berlin had summer homes on Queens's shores. Now it's a less-expensive-than-Manhattan "outer borough," used as a staging area for upward mobility by ambitious newcomers poised to make their move either to the 'burbs or Manhattan.

Still, as a Buddhist once told me, "All is change." So the gastronomes better get here quick before the gentrification of western Queens displaces ethnic establishments with upscale eateries purveying bland, ostentatiously garnished imitations of the real thing.

If music is the language of love,

food is at least the language of tolerance. In South Asia, Pakistan and India may be threatening each other with nukes, but in Jackson Heights they're all shopping in the same stores. Similarly, Arabs and Israelis find common ground buying chick-peas and tabbouleh in Middle Eastern specialty stores. And whether you call it Greek or Turkish coffee, you can find what you're looking for at Titan Foods in Astoria.

The thing about Queens, though, is that the guy in the back isn't always someone who came over on the boat (or plane) with the guy in the front. Often immigrant businesses have no qualms about hiring more recent immigrants from whatever labor pool is willing to work cheap. Thus an immigrant from one culture becomes intimately acquainted with the intricacies of another's cuisine by working in the kitchen. Often these same individuals buy the business, or open a similar one of their own.

The superficial trappings may be the same, but with vestiges of the new owner's culture infiltrating the one advertised. Or, inversely, an immigrant may open a business reflective of his/her background but influenced by the time spent with "outsiders."

Examples of the phenomenon abound in Queens. You want good bagels? You can find them at a Thai bagel bakery that sells Thai specialties on the side. French pastry? Choose between Indian or Korean bakers. Here you can either choose your Chinese food by province or sample Chinese food that caters to a Latino, Indian, or kosher palate. Italian?—try the Croatians (or is it the other way around?). Wander into what looks to the naked eye to be an ordinary pizza place; the pizza may be subpar, but you can get great falafel, empanadas, or Brazilian appetizers, depending. The list goes on and on.

All this makes for a happy

hunting ground for those with a passion for variety. This book will assist the reader in locating its quarry—something unusual and delicious to eat.

When it comes to multiculturalism, Queens may be taking the lead, but the rest of America is not far behind. Immigrant communities are springing up all over the USA, creating mini-Queenses everywhere. Even if you're not within striking distance of Queens, there's sure to be some emerging ethnic community where you are. The information provided here about ethnic foods and customs will guide you in making informed choices about how and what to sample in your own explorations.

This book is not meant to be an encyclopedia of all cuisines or all Queens restaurants. Based on a cursory scan of the Queens Yellow Pages, there are approximately 3,000 Queens eateries. Explanations of cuisines were included or omitted based on three criteria. First, would the average American have difficulty figuring out how or what to order? European cuisines were omitted on the grounds that mainstream America is familiar enough with their offerings and customs to make

guidance unnecessary. Italian food, for example, needs no explanation.

Next, does a significant immigrant community of a given ethnicity exist in Queens, judging from census statistics and fieldwork? Finally, if a group is exotic enough, and represents enough critical mass to form a community, has it opened any businesses in Queens offering its traditional fare? For example, even though 20,742 Queensites reported their ancestry as "sub-Saharan African," none of them seem to have contributed to the Queens culinary scene in any detectable way. They must all eat in the Bronx, where there are a number of African eateries.

All of the above is, of course, in a constant state of flux. You will be shooting at a moving target. This book is not an exhaustive directory or Queens eateries, but a guide to some that are regarded as either outstanding or unique in what they offer. Use this book for inspiration as well as information, and after sampling from some of the places described herein, go out and be the first to discover the newest arrivals. Just bring an adventurous spirit and a hearty appetite.

East Asia

⊙ CHINA

WHEN I WAS GROWING UP IN QUEENS, MY family frequently ate what we then regarded as Chinese food. Pre-1970s Queens Chinese food was Cantonese, and invariably limited to a few tried-and-true favorites like chow mein, fried rice, and barbecued spare ribs.

If there were other things on the menu, our family ignored them. Our fellow diners were also "round-eyes."

As an adult, I began to experiment with the varied Chinese dishes offered by Manhattan's more sophisticated Chinese restaurants. A course in Chinese cooking given by the China Institute also opened my eyes to the broad range of culinary wonders under the umbrella of Chinese cuisine.

While I was educating my palate in Manhattan, large numbers of Chinese immigrants were moving to Queens. A Chinatown sprang up in Flushing, distinctly different from its Manhattan counterpart.

Flushing's streets, compared with those in lower Manhattan, are spacious, and there was room to build. Consequently, a cleaner, more middle-class Chinatown emerged, shared by a broad spectrum of East Asian cultures. According to 2000 census figures, there are 139,820 Chinese Americans in Queens—40 percent of New York's Chinese population.

Chinese immigrants have continued to settle throughout Queens in large numbers. In the new millennium, it has become more difficult to find an old-style Cantonese restaurant catering to a Western clientele than it is to find an ethnic or regional one. In the

KUNAN LAM PREPARING FOOD AT HONG KONG DRAGON BOAT
FESTIVAL HELD ANNUALLY AT FLUSHING MEADOWS PARK

Queens of today, the appropriate response to the question "Would you like to have Chinese food tonight?" would be "What kind?"

Chinese is one of the great cuisines of the world, right up there with French. Food is such a fundamental part of the Chinese culture that the question "Have you eaten?" is the equivalent of "How are you?" to North Americans. It's just a pro forma inquiry that does not require a truthful, detailed answer. Simply answer "Yes" even if you haven't actually eaten.

Regional Chinese styles are about as different from one another as a New England boiled dinner is from a Cajun jambalaya or a Tex-Mex burrito. Chinese cuisines have certain things in common, but their differences can be extreme.

When dining in Chinese restaurants that cater to an ethnic clientele, sometimes you will be steered away from dishes that the server believes Westerners will not like, or the restaurant will prepare a toned-down version of a spicy dish. If you are an adventurous eater, be insistent about what you want. If you shy away from novel foods, your server is probably right. If you like spicy food, tell your server you want your food to be "ma la." That means "spicy." Having a little knowledge of Chinese etiquette can't hurt in ingratiating yourself with the establishment. Here are some pointers.

Chinese tea is normally served throughout the meal. You should always top up the cups of those around you before topping up your own. To thank one another for the courtesy, you will often see the Chinese tapping the first two fingers of the right hand on the table. This gesture dates back to the time of the Qing dynasty, when a certain emperor was fond of wandering incognito among his people. Since his companions could not kowtow to the emperor without revealing his identity, they devised the finger tapping as an inconspicuous substitute. It's also quite practical because one can continue to talk and tap his fingers at the same time.

The Chinese use wooden chopsticks for eating and a porcelain spoon for soup. When finished, set your chopsticks on the table or on the chopstick rest provided. Placing them parallel on top of your bowl is considered a sign of bad luck. You must not stick your chopsticks upright in a bowl of rice. This has too much of a resemblance to incense burning in a bowl of sand, used in ceremonies for the dead. And you must not wave your chopsticks or use them to point at people, as you can easily poke someone in the eye. It is also impolite to cross over someone else's chopsticks when reaching for food.

When eating rice, it is customary to hold the bowl close to your mouth.

Serving dishes are not passed around; instead, you should reach for food using the opposite end of your chopsticks (not the end you put in your mouth).

Turning a fish over on its plate is considered a bad omen, since it represents the capsizing of a boat. Instead, the fish bone should be removed from the top to get at the flesh underneath. You can always leave this to the server.

The serving of fruit signifies the end of the meal. Once the meal is over, you are expected to leave promptly. This is contrary to the Western custom of lingering over a cup of coffee. In fact, most Chinese restaurants will not even serve coffee, so here's your hat, what's your hurry?

WHEN DINING WITH A CHINESE HOST OR AT A BANQUET

Never begin to eat or drink before your host.

At a banquet, eat lightly in the beginning, since there could be up to 20 courses served. Expect your host to fill your bowl when you empty it. Finishing all your food may be an insult to your host, indicating that your host did not provide you with enough food. But leaving a bowl completely full is also rude. Never take the last piece of food on a platter.

Before you begin to explore the differences, there are some basic commonalities to all Chinese cuisine. Since all Chinese eat with chopsticks, Chinese food is almost always cut up by the food preparer, or occasionally by the server during presentation.

Tea is the beverage of choice throughout China. At every restaurant, a pot of tea arrives with the menus. Grocery stores sell dozens of kinds of tea in colorful cans and boxes. Tea shops may offer more than 50 varieties, some for everyday drinking, some—very expensive—for connoisseurs.

TEA

Tea is a beverage, a health enhancer, and a social custom. It was enjoyed throughout China by the seventh or eighth century, and is as deeply intertwined with Chinese history as its art or literature. People have gathered to socialize in teahouses since at least the Song dynasty (960-1279). Poets wrote in them and about them. Artists painted them.

Tea is still China's most valuable agricultural crop. All tea is made from the leaves of the same plant, *Camellia sinensis,* a relative of the familiar flowering camellia. Differences in climate, soil, and processing influence the flavor. Green tea is made by drying the hand-picked leaves with heat. Black tea, called red tea in China, is made by crushing the leaves a little to bruise them, then allowing them to "ferment" (actually, oxidize) before drying. Oolong tea is also fermented, but for less time. Here are a few readily available kinds of tea:

Gunpowder (Pingshuizhu): a strong-flavored green tea. During the drying process, the leaves are rolled into tiny pellets. They unfold in hot water. This tea contains fluoride, and in China is considered good for teeth.

Jasmine (Moli hua): green tea dried together with fragrant jasmine flowers, a favorite in Beijing.

Keemun (Qihong): a high-quality black tea. Black teas are most popular in South China.

Lichee (Lichi): black tea treated with juice from lichee fruit, which adds a delicious, fruity flavor.

Lung Ching (Longjing), Dragon Well: a famous green tea, which makes a beautiful beverage with a mellow flavor. Green teas are especially popular in hot weather.

Pu-erh (Pu'er): an earthy oolong; it soothes indigestion.

Tieh Kwan Yin (Tie guanyin): a mellow oolong, named after the Buddhist Goddess of Mercy.

BUBBLE TEA

In the 1980s bubble tea, a trendy new drink especially popular with the young, originated in Taiwan and rapidly gained acceptance throughout Hong Kong and China. Not long after, it arrived in Queens.

Bubble tea is a cool, refreshing, sweet drink with tapioca pearls sitting on the bottom of a clear cup. It is drunk through a jumbo straw, wide enough to accommodate the tapioca pearls. It usually includes a healthy tea infused with a flavoring. Sometimes the drink is made with fresh fruit, milk, and crushed ice to create a healthy milkshake.

Tapioca pearls are usually black, but can sometimes be white or transparent. Depending on the ingredients of the pearl, the color may vary. The white and translucent pearls are made of caramel, starch, and chamomile root extract. The black pearl includes sweet potato, cassava root, and brown sugar. The consistency of tapioca pearls is somewhere between Jell-O and chewing gum. They are the size of a pea. Bubble tea is also known as the "boba" drink in Western China because it is described as having the same texture as female breasts.

WHERE TO GO FOR TEA IN QUEENS

Ten Ren Tea
135-18 Roosevelt Ave., Flushing
Subway: No. 7 to Main St.
718-461-9305

An international chain ("The Art of Chinese Tea") on Roosevelt, just before Prince. In addition to bubble tea, they sell exquisite Chinese tea varieties, both loose and bagged, such as oolong, green, jasmine, white, pouchong, and blends. The classic tea ceremony is sometimes demonstrated at the store. A ceremony can be arranged for a party of 12-15 people.

FOR BUBBLE TEA

While bubble tea is enjoyed by people of all ages, cafes specializing in bubble tea occupy somewhat the same place in Chinese culture as ice cream parlors. They are especially frequented by the young.

Relax Tea House
39-07 Prince Street (corner of Prince St. and 39th Ave.), Flushing
718-888-1488
Subway: No. 7 to Main St.
Bubble tea and Hong Kong diner food. A trendy place with an extensive variety of bubble teas and many amusingly weird Chinese interpretations of Western food.

Sago Tea Cafe
39-02 Main St., Flushing
718-353-2899
Subway: No. 7 to Main St.

> ## LU YU SAID IN THE CLASSIC ART OF TEA
> "Tea tempers the spirit, harmonizes the mind, dispels lassitude and relieves fatigue, awakens the thought and prevents drowsiness."

Ice cream parlor atmosphere. Lots of kids.

Flushing Mall
133-31 39th Ave., (between College Point Blvd. and Prince St.) Flushing
Subway: No. 7 to Main St.
Once inside this mall, it is easy to believe you've been transported to Asia. There are several bubble tea vendors both in the food court area and interspersed among other types of vendors throughout the mall.

Sweet-n-Tart
136-11 38th Ave., Flushing
718-661-3380
Subway: No. 7 to Main St.
Bubble tea; fruity, healthy concoctions; and Hong Kong-style Cantonese food and dim sum.

BREAKFAST
Breakfast foods are pretty universal throughout the various regions of

China. One of the most popular Chinese breakfast foods is jook, or congee. It originated in the southeastern province of Fukien, but is now eaten all over China. Congee is a porridge made by slow-cooking rice in about ten times the normal amount of water with odd bits of meat or seafood and other ingredients like raw peanuts or duck eggs. Since the jook itself is pretty bland, the additions and garnishes are what make the dish. The Chinese eat jook for breakfast, but also throughout the day, and as a late-night snack. Another popular breakfast item is the Chinese doughnut. It comes sweet or unsweet and, except for its elongated shape, is similar to a large, heavy American doughnut.

WHERE TO FIND AN AUTHENTIC CHINESE BREAKFAST

King Five Noodle of Elmhurst
(premises formerly occupied by Captain King)
82-39 Broadway, Elmhurst
718-205-7888
Subway: G, R, V to Elmhurst Ave.
Excellent Chinese breakfast on weekends from 9–11 a.m.

King 5 Noodle House

39-07 Prince St., 1G, Flushing
718 888-1268
Subway: No. 7 to Main St.; north on Main St. to 39th Ave.; west on 39th Ave.

East Manor Buffet & Restaurant
42-07 Main St., Flushing
718-353-6333
Subway: No. 7 to Flushing-Main St.

East Manor Buffet & Restaurant
79-17 Albion Ave., Elmhurst
718-803-3952
Subway: G, R, V to Grand Ave.
Chinese breakfast daily in takeout area (small, pleasant seating area for eat-in) from 11 a.m.

Flushing Mall
133-31 39th Ave., Flushing
(between College Point Blvd. and Prince St.)
Subway: No. 7 to Main St.; north on Main St. to 39th Ave.; west on 39th Ave.
Several of the food court vendors offer Chinese breakfast specialties.

DIM SUM

Literally meaning "to touch your heart," dim sum consists of a variety of dumplings, steamed dishes, and other goodies such as the famous egg custard tarts. Dim sum straddles the gap between

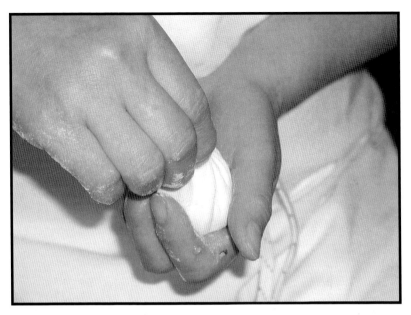

PREPARING BUNS FOR STEAMING

breakfast and lunch, usually being served between 11 a.m. and 3 p.m.

Dim sum first made an appearance in this country in the 19th century, brought by Chinese immigrants—most of whom were from the Canton region—settling on the east and west coasts. Some believe that dim sum inspired the whole idea of brunch; the word brunch came into usage only in the late 1800s. (Some also believe that the western sandwich—the quintessential cowboy snack—came about when a Chinese cook tried to adapt egg foo yung to suit Western tastes.)

Originally a Cantonese custom, dim sum is inextricably linked to the Chinese tradition of yum cha, or drinking tea. Travelers journeying along the famous Silk Road needed a place to rest, so teahouses began springing up along the roadside. Rural farmers, exhausted after long hours working in the fields, would also head to the local teahouse for an afternoon of tea and relaxing conversation. Still, it took several centuries for the culinary art of dim sum to develop.

It was once considered inappropriate to combine tea with food—in fact, a famous 3rd-century imperial physician claimed this would lead to excessive weight gain.

	CANTONESE	MANDARIN
STEAMED DIM SUM		
Barbecued Pork Bun	Char Siu Bao	Cha Shao Bao
Chinese Chive Dumpling	Gow Choy Gau	Jia Chai Jiao
Chiu Chow Dumpling	Chiu Chow Fun Guok	Chao Zhou Fen Jiao
Pork Dumpling	Siu Mai	Shao Mai
Pork Rib with Salted Black Beans	Jing Pie Gwut	Zhen Pai Guo
Rice in Lotus Leaf	Naw Mai Gai	Nao MiJi
Rice Noodle Roll (beef, shrimp, or BBQ pork)	Churn Fun	Zhen Chung Fen
Shrimp Dumpling	Ha Gau	Xia Jiao
DEEP-FRIED DIM SUM		
Flaky Taro Dumpling	Woo Gok	Yu Jiao
Glutinous Rice Dumpling	Horn Soi Gok	Xian Sui Jiao
Shrimp Toast	Ha Daw-See	Gang Su Xia Daw-See
Spring Roll	Chun Guen	Chun Juan
SWEET DIM SUM		
Black Sesame Seed Roll	Gee Mar Guen	Zhi Ma Juan
Egg Custard Tart	Don Tot	Dan Tak
Sesame Seed Ball	Jin Dui	Jan Dui
Steamed Sponge Cake	Ma Lai Gough	Xhen Song Guao
Water Chestnut Cake	Ma Tai Gough	Ma Tii Guao

However, as tea's ability to aid in digestion and cleanse the palate became known, teahouse proprietors began adding a variety of snacks, and the tradition of dim sum was born.

Today, dim sum is served throughout China, particularly in Shanghai. Better still, it's widely available throughout Queens, and popping up in many locations throughout the U.S.

Noon is probably the optimum time to arrive at a restaurant for dim sum. The etiquette is simple: Most teahouses or restaurants have large round tables that can accommodate 10-12 diners. The optimum dim sum experience is to dine with a large group so you can sample the most varieties. If your party is small, and the restaurant is busy, you may be seated at a table shared by others. If your accidental dining partners happen to be Chinese, English-speaking, and friendly, this can be a real plus. The dim sum are brought around on carts, with the servers pausing at each table and displaying the dishes. If the server does not speak English, all you need to do is nod if something looks appealing. You will be served, and a notation will be made on your check for each item you accept.

The trick to enjoying dim sum, which I have never personally mastered, is to pace yourself. Invariably, after I'm stuffed to the gills, feeling like I won't be eating again for a week, a parade of carts passes by with such enticing offerings that I mentally slap my forehead, wondering why I couldn't have waited just a little longer to fill myself up. There is actually a proper sequence in which dim sum should be consumed, although it's been my experience that your time of arrival, and which carts are circulating, has more to do with what you are offered first. Restaurants also tend to push the deep-fried items when they see Westerners, thinking that this is what we prefer.

THERE ARE MANY FABULOUS SPOTS FOR DIM SUM IN QUEENS. HERE ARE A FEW OF MY FAVORITES

East Lake
42-33 Main St. (at Franklin Ave.),
Flushing
718-539-8532
Subway: No. 7 to Main St.; walk
south to Franklin Ave.

Ocean Jewel Seafood Restaurant
133-30 39th Ave., Flushing (across
street from Flushing Mall)
718-359-8603
Subway: No. 7 to Main St.

Fay Da
41-60 Main St., Flushing
718-886-4568
Subway: No. 7 to Main St.; walk
south on Main St.

Gum Fung Restaurant
136-28 39th Ave., Flushing
718-762-8821
Subway: No. 7 to Main St.; walk
north to 39th Ave.; right on 39th
Ave. about one block

Chinese cuisine can be roughly
classified into four main regional
styles with numerous subcategories:

CANTONESE
(GUANDONG)

The most familiar to Westerners,
this light, fresh-tasting cuisine
emphasizes fowl and meat, and is
usually accompanied by rice. Quick
cooking techniques like steaming
and stir-frying are most frequently
used to preserve the ingredients'
natural flavors. Guandong chefs also
pay attention to the artistic
presentation of their dishes. Roasted
and barbecued meats became
favorites at restaurants and meat
shops because traditional Chinese
kitchens did not have ovens.

FOR CANTONESE IN QUEENS

> **FOOD SYMBOLISM**
> An honored guest will be
> served a snapper's head or
> shell to hail him and show a
> warm welcome in some
> districts.

All the spots listed for dim sum also
serve great Cantonese food. If you
really want to eat yourself into
oblivion, here are two highly
recommended buffet-style
restaurants that serve up a dizzying
array of Cantonese specialties and
other fare such as sushi, Beijing
duck, and, really, you name it. What
sets them apart from most all-you-
can-eat buffets is that instead of
steamer trays replenished from the
kitchen, they serve from preparation
stations. These restaurants are vast,
and everything they serve is
impeccably fresh.

East Manor Buffet & Restaurant
42-07 Main St., Flushing
718-353-6333
Subway: No. 7 to Flushing-Main
St.

East Manor Buffet & Restaurant
79-17 Albion Ave., Elmhurst
718-803-3952
Subway: G, R, V to Grand Ave.

ORNAMENTS IN FLUSHING FOR DECKING THE HALLS IN CHINESE NEW YEAR

FOR HONG KONG-STYLE CANTONESE

Ping's Seafood
83-02 Queens Blvd., Elmhurst,
718-396-1238
Subway: G, R, V to Grand Ave.
The emphasis is on seafood here.
The neon light show on the roof
alone makes it worth the visit.

SICHUAN

The word Sichuan means "four
rivers," and there are four main
rivers in this landlocked province.
Characterized by its spicy and
pungent flavors, Sichuan cuisine,
with a myriad of tastes, emphasizes
the use of hot peppers. Pepper and
Sichuan peppercorns (hua jiao, the
tongue-numbing berries of the
prickly ash) are included in the
majority of Sichuan dishes. It is
illegal, by the way, to import
Chinese peppercorns into this
country, as they can carry a disease
that can infect citrus crops.
Purveyors of Chinese ingredients
seem to be selling them under the
counter to trusted customers,
claiming that they are drawing on
existing supplies. Garlic, ginger, and
fermented soybean are essential in
the cooking process. Wild vegetables

and meats are often chosen as ingredients, while frying, frying without oil, pickling, and braising are basic Sichuan cooking techniques.

Lack of access to the sea did not hinder this province; its fertile hills and valleys provide a bounty of crops, including tea, rice, corn, sweet potatoes, wheat, rape, sugar cane, peanuts, and bamboo. The province is also rich with groves of orange, tangerine, pear, star fruit, litchi trees, plantations of bananas, and many, many herbs. It was here, during the Tang and Sung dynasties, that local people developed the habit of drinking tea, a custom that spread to other parts of China.

Perhaps the best-known Sichuan dish is mapo doufu. The name actually means "pockmarked lady

tofu," a not very tactful reference to the appearance of its originator. Other well-known Sichuan favorites include hot and sour soup, dan dan noodles, dry-fried string beans, tea-smoked duck, kung bao chicken, and beef with tangerine peel. Any dish with "strange taste" in the name means that it's salty, sweet, hot, numbing, and sour all together. The works.

Food from the province of Yunnan is often regarded as a subcategory of Sichuan cuisine. Its most noteworthy dish is yu nan noodles. Its colloquial Chinese name may be loosely translated as "noodles over the bridge." The legend is that it was created by a farmer's wife whose husband always complained that the lunch she brought to his distant field was cold and not fresh. Instead of telling him to go buy his lunch at Mickey Dee's, she came up with an ingenious solution. She heated chicken broth in an earthenware pot until it was intensely hot, and poured oil over its surface. Then she carried the soup and thinly sliced raw ingredients separately to the field where her husband was toiling. There she added the raw ingredients to the broth, which retained its heat because of the layer of oil. The hot broth cooked the raw ingredients, and her husband was satisfied that his meal was both hot and fresh. Perhaps this was the earliest form of take-out.

When you order yu nan noodles, a scalding mini-cauldron of soup is brought to the table, accompanied by a platter of thinly sliced shrimp, salmon, pork liver, sea cucumber, scallops, mushrooms, white chives, pea sprouts, and baby spinach. There is also a bowl of chewy rice noodles that resemble very white spaghetti. You slip the raw ingredients into the hot broth, fish and meat first, wait a few minutes for them to cook, and then place some noodles in your bowl. Next, skim the oil from the top of the broth and discard it, and ladle the soup and its contents into your bowl. The broth is both delicate and flavorful, and the ingredients retain their flavor because of the brief cooking time. This dish is the specialty of only one restaurant in Queens: the Yuan Garden in the Sheraton LaGuardia Hotel.

FOR SICHUAN FOOD

Spicy & Tasty and Sichuan Dynasty have terrific food for the gastronomic adventurer. Some of the animal parts listed on the menu may be off-putting to the squeamish. The restaurants seem to tone down the heat for non-ethnics. If you like really spicy food, ask for it to be made "ma la" and carry a fire extinguisher.

Spicy & Tasty
39-07 Prince St. 1H, Flushing
718-359-1601
Subway: No. 7 to Main St.

Sichuan Dynasty
135-32 40th Rd., Flushing
718-961-7500
Subway: No. 7 to Main St.
Sichuan Dynasty also offers Sichuan fire pot, the four-alarm version of the hot pot.

FOR YU NAN NOODLES

The Yuan Garden is a particularly elegant Chinese restaurant for Queens, located in the Sheraton LaGuardia Hotel. It caters largely to the Asian business travelers who stay there. It has underground parking and a concourse with upscale Asian shops. You feel like you've landed somewhere in Asia.

Yuan Garden Restaurant
Sheraton LaGuardia Hotel
135-20 39th Ave., Flushing
718-460-6666
Subway: No. 7 to Main St.

WATCHING FOR THE JADE RABBIT

The Moon Festival usually takes place in September, when the full moon is at its brightest. The date of the Chinese Moon Festival is on the 15th moon day of the 8th Chinese lunar month (chicken month.) If you watch the moon on the Chinese Moon Festival night, you should feel that it's fuller than in previous years (assuming you remember how bright it was in previous years).

The festival probably originated as a harvest celebration. Later it became associated with the legend of Chang E. She was exiled to the moon after swallowing the magic potion of long life. If you look closely at the moon, you may be able to see the Jade Rabbit. He keeps Chang E, the Moon Lady, company.

During the Yuan dynasty (A.D. 1280–1368), China was ruled by the Mongolian people. Leaders from the preceding Sung dynasty (A.D. 960–1280) were unhappy at submitting to foreign rule, and devised a plan to coordinate a rebellion without it being discovered. Knowing that the Moon Festival was drawing near, they ordered the making of special cakes. Baked into each moon cake was a message with the outline of the attack. On the night of the Moon Festival, the rebels successfully attacked and overthrew the government. What followed was the establishment of the Ming dynasty (A.D. 1368–1644).

Because the full moon is round and symbolizes reunion, the Mid-Autumn Festival is also known as the festival of reunion. Chinese families get together to eat moon cakes, watch the moon, and sing moon poems on the Moon Festival night. It is a comfort to Chinese people who are separated from their friends or loved ones to know that they are sharing the same moon on this special night. It is customary to give decorative boxes of moon cakes—pastries with sweet, dense fillings—as gifts at this time of year.

Chinese bakeries and food purveyors do a brisk business in moon cakes this time of year. Moon cake styles vary by region. The Taiwanese type is made with green bean paste, or with salted egg yolk, red kidney bean paste, and lotus paste. The Peking style is filled with a slightly smoky-tasting prune paste. Those of Suzhou are similar to shortbread and have several layers containing bean paste and ginkgo-spiced salt or meat, usually pork. Cantonese moon cakes are formed in molds with Chinese characters on them, perhaps an allusion to the Sung dynasty attack, although now usually representing the name of the bakery. The most popular fillings are red bean paste, lotus paste, and nuts and seeds. Some have a whole cooked duck egg yolk inside to represent the moon. Some Chinese insist that cooked taro be included because at the time of creation, taro was the first food discovered at night in the moonlight.

This is a joyous holiday, meant to remind its celebrants of what's right with the world.

SHANGHAI

Shanghai is located in the temperate basin of the Yangtze River, which is dotted with rivers and lakes, and abounds in local produce. Shanghai food features vegetable and seafood dishes with stew-in-brown-soybean and stir-fry-in-vegetable-oil as the main cooking methods.

The use of sugar is integral to Shanghaiese cuisine and, especially when used in combination with soy sauce, infuses foods and sauces with a taste that is not so much sweet as savory. A typical Shanghai household will consume sugar at the same rate as soy sauce, even without pastry baking. Non-natives tend to have difficulty identifying this usage of sugar, and are often surprised when told of the "secret ingredient." Another characteristic is the use of a great variety of seafood. Rice is preferred over noodles and other wheat products.

The Shanghaiese dish that always wows "round eyes" is xiao long bao (little dragon bun). These delicate morsels are tiny dumplings filled with meat and broth. Sometimes they will be listed on menus simply as "steamed tiny buns." Ask for soup dumplings, and they'll know what you mean. Lift them from the steamer with tongs or chopsticks, dip them in the accompanying sauce, and place them on your spoon. Then take a tiny bite, suck out the broth, and enjoy the rest. Some restaurants don't prepare the dipping sauce, but instead provide the ingredients for you to prepare your own. If this is the case, mix soy sauce, vinegar, and

ASSORTED MOONCAKES

sesame oil to taste. Some people like to add a dash of hot sauce.

Beggar's chicken is a legendary dish wrapped in lotus leaves, covered in clay, and oven-baked to steamy, tasty perfection—in olden times, it was baked in the ground. Lime-and-ginger-flavored "1,000-year-old" eggs, those snack eggs that are boiled forever, are also popular.

Another well-known Shanghaiese-style of preparation uses alcohol. Fish, eel, crab, and chicken are "drunken" with spirits and served raw or parboiled. Salted meats and preserved vegetables are also commonly used to spice up this dish.

FOR SHANGHAIESE SPECIALTIES

Joe's Shanghai
136-21 37th Ave., Flushing
718-539-3838
Subway: No. 7 to Main St.

Yangtze River Restaurant
135-21 40th Rd., Flushing
646-996-7632
Subway: No. 7 to Main St.

BEIJING

History and climate conspired to play key roles in the evolution of Beijing cuisine. In an area with hot, dry summers and bitterly cold winters, food that is both substantial and nourishing is demanded. Instead of rice, wheat is the staple grain in the north, and noodles made from wheat flour are central to many meals. This culinary tradition combines the features of Qing dynasty court dishes, Moslem cuisine, and Mongolian tastes.

Beijing food can be eaten in a surprising variety of ways. Beijing chefs place heavy emphasis on cooking time and slicing techniques, and they strive for bland tastes and soft and tender textures.

The Mongolian rulers of the Yuan dynasty introduced mutton. It is said that Mongolian soldiers would fill their helmets with water, then boil whatever beef and mutton was available. They would season and cook their meats to their liking. This style of cooking eventually spread to other regions, and each dynasty changed or refined it in some way.

Beijing was the gathering place of the literati and officials, and many skilled chefs followed these people to Beijing. These chefs brought different cuisines to the capital and greatly enriched the flavors of Beijing cooking, making it the cosmopolitan melting pot of Chinese cuisine.

BEIJING SPECIALTIES

Noodles, pancakes, and bread are popular in the north. Pancakes are an essential part of two of its most widely known dishes: Beijing (Peking) duck and mu shu pork. The crisp skin of Beijing duck is its most prized part. Pieces of roast duck are wrapped in thin pancakes with scallions, cucumber, turnip, and plum sauce. Mu shu pork consists of marinated pork stir-fried with other Chinese vegetables and eaten in a similar manner to Beijing duck, wrapped in pancakes with hoisin sauce.

Hot pot: A giant communal pot of slowly simmering stock is placed in the center of the table. Diners are given a variety of raw, thinly sliced meats (lamb, beef, fish, poultry, etc.) and vegetables. They immerse pieces of their food into the simmering stock, cook it to their liking, and, if desired, dip the food into one of a selection of condiments. After the food is cooked, the rich broth is consumed by any who have room for it. The hot pot feast, called wei-lu, means to circle a pot, which symbolizes family unity and togetherness by evoking the image of a family gathered around a pot. **Dumplings, noodles, and breads** are favored over rice in Beijing. Because of the city's northern location, its food tends to be hearty, in order to keep the human body warm. **Steamed bread,** or mantou, is famous in the north. Mantou is made of flour and so is white in color. It doesn't have any particular flavor.

Guo bu li are a famous type of stuffed steamed buns that originated in Tianjin. A seller of steamed buns (gou-zu) named Bo-zu invented a special recipe for the dough that made it soft but not greasy. Bo-zu's gou-zu became so popular that his customers teased him that he had no time to socialize (li-jen) any more. People started to call him Gou-Bu-Li (Gou-Zu Not Social). You will find these delicacies stuffed with pork, lamb, vegetables, red bean, or with combinations of any of these fillings.

We've come across two types of **hand-drawn noodles** in Queens. There is lan chu, the type that starts with a ball of dough that is miraculously folded, pulled, and swung overhead repeatedly like a jump rope until it magically forms skeins of noodles. The other type of handmade noodles are flat, squarish noodles called Shangxi dow shiaw. Named for their city of origin and the process by which they are made, these noodles are made by shaving pieces from a ball of dough with a special cutter.

FOR NORTHERN CHINESE SPECIALTIES IN QUEENS

For fantastic hot pot, either incendiary or mellow (or a combination of the two), the place to go is Happy Family. The owner was specially trained by a Mongolian master. It also serves fabulous lamb dumplings and other lamb specialties.

Little Lamb Happy Family Restaurant
36-35 Main St., Flushing
718-358-6667
Subway: No. 7 to Main St.

For Xinjiang-style barbecued lamb and goat, including some way–out specialties like goat's eyeballs:

A Fan Ti
136-80 41st Ave., Flushing
718-358-7925
Subway: No. 7 to Main St.

For handmade noodles, or gou bu li:

Gou-Bu-Li
135-28 40th Rd., Flushing
718-886-2121
Subway: No. 7 to Main St.

To watch handmade noodles being prepared with great aplomb, visit the Hand Drawn Noodles vendor in the food court of the Flushing Mall.

Hand-Drawn Noodle
Booth #C26, Food Court, Flushing Mall
133-31 39th Ave., Flushing
(between College Point Blvd. and Prince St.)
Subway: No. 7 to Main St.

For great, unbelievably cheap steamed buns, dumplings, and wonton soup (ask for the "big" wonton soup"), head for a counter and a few tables within a larger with its entrance on 41st Street. The sign on 41st Street says:

Shan Dong Dumpling House
41-28 Main St., Flushing
718-930-6000 (don't bother calling unless you speak Mandarin)
Subway: No. 7 to Main St.

TAIWANESE

Here's where things get even more complicated. A significant proportion of Queens's Chinese population, especially those well established enough to open businesses, is Taiwanese. While it draws heavily on mainland influences, Taiwanese cuisine is something of a cuisine unto itself.

There are several distinct populations in Taiwan, each with its own cuisine. There are the "native Taiwanese," the descendants of the settlers who arrived 350 or more years ago and intermarried with the indigenous Malay-Polynesian population. They nicknamed themselves "sweet potatoes," both after the vegetable, which is popular with the Taiwanese, and the shape of their island. There are the mainlanders, referred to as "taros" by the locals, who emigrated to Taiwan between 1945 and 1949, mostly from

Shanghai and the Fujian coast. There is the Hakka population, originally a central Chinese people who were dispersed throughout southeastern China and Taiwan 900 years ago, and who still retain their own distinct language and culture. Finally there are the indigenous mountain people of Malay-Polynesian descent, a tiny fraction of the population.

The emphasis in Taiwanese cooking is on light, natural flavors and freshness, and there is no pursuit of complex flavors. In addition to the ever-present soy sauce, rice wine, and sesame oil, Taiwanese cuisine relies on an abundant array of seasonings: fermented black beans, pickled radishes, peanuts, chili peppers, parsley, and a local variety of basil ("nine-story tower").

You won't find combo dishes like beef with broccoli; Taiwanese food tends to separate ingredients. Most Taiwanese dishes emphasize one ingredient, be it meat, seafood, or a vegetable. For a balanced meal, you should order an assortment of dishes representing each category, and a soup. Taiwanese food works best family-style.

San pei chicken, literally meaning "three-cup chicken," is a popular traditional chicken dish. The oral history of the dish recounts that one cup each of soy sauce, rice wine, and sesame oil were placed in an earthenware pot on low heat at dawn before a day of work in the fields. By dusk, the dish had simmered into a delightful stew flavored with nine-story tower, and eaten with either rice or congee.

Chou tofu, aka "stinky tofu," is a favorite food of the Taiwanese. Yep, it smells, but just think of it as the Eastern equivalent of a really ripe cheese. Regarded in that context, maybe the smell isn't so bad. It has a pleasantly tart flavor, a crisply fried exterior, and a smooth interior.

To prepare stinky tofu, cooks start with a brine made with a combination of long-fermented vegetables such as amaranth, mustard greens, bamboo shoots, and Chinese herbs. (Adventurous cooks add shrimp heads and fish stomach for added zest.) A noxious smell some days later signals that the brine is ready. That's when tofu squares are marinated in the brine. Due to a chemical reaction caused by microorganisms, the marinating bean curd develops a unique, spongy consistency, for which it is prized as much as for its flavor. The tofu is cut into chunks that are deep-fried and served with pickled cabbage. Some connoisseurs of stinky tofu say the magic is in the topping, which is made of soy sauce, vinegar, and chili oil.

TO SAMPLE STINKY TOFU AND OTHER TAIWANESE DELIGHTS IN QUEENS, TRY

David's Taiwanese Gourmet
84-02 Broadway, Elmhurst
718-429-4818
Subway: G, R, V to Elmhurst Ave.

Laifood
38-18 Prince St., Flushing
718-321-0653
Subway: No. 7 to Main St.

Main Street Taiwanese Gourmet
59-14A Main St., Flushing
718-886-8788
Subway: No. 7 to Main St.

Flushing Mall
133-31 39th Ave. (between College
Point Blvd. and Prince St.)
Subway: No. 7 to Main St.

HAKKA

The Hakka are descended from migratory tribes of ethnic Han people, who came from central China. Their ancestors exiled themselves from foreign rulers like the Mongols in the Yuan dynasty. Originally a central Chinese population known to live in mostly hilly areas, the Hakka wandered south in several waves, most during or just after the fall of the Song dynasty in 1279. To distinguish these mountain folk from other immigrants in the area, the Cantonese dubbed them "Hakka." That name translates as "guest people" or "stranger people," and it has stayed with them even though their guest status goes back more than 900 years.

Hakka people are noted for their preservation of cultural characteristics that can be traced to the pre-Qin period (about 2200 years ago) as expressed in customs, foods, spoken language, etc. Once migrants within China, Hakka families now reside all over the world. In fact, several generations of Hakka have lived in countries like Cambodia, Malaysia, India, Thailand, Jamaica, Hong Kong, Singapore, and Taiwan. Others live in North America, South America, and Europe, and are often the group that introduced Chinese cuisine to these countries and that still owns many of the Chinese restaurants.

When the Hakka migrated to southern China, fresh produce was at a premium, forcing them to heavily utilize dried and preserved ingredients, like onion and various kinds of fermented bean curd. Because the hill country is so far

CANTONESE BARBECUE

inland, seafood was a rarity in their diet. Pork, though scarce, was by far the most favored meat of the Hakkas. They were known as able farmers and frugal people who knew how to make use of every part of the pig.

As of this writing, the only Hakka restaurant in Queens has closed. Be on the lookout for a replacement.

OVERSEAS CHINESE

Chinese food is enjoyed in almost every country outside of China. Just as chicken chow mein is a dish invented outside of China to please

local palates, Chinese chefs have embraced local ingredients and sensibilities in their offerings wherever they've gone.

The only type of "overseas Chinese" that is disappearing is the American variety. You'd be hard-pressed to find an old-fashioned American-style Chinese restaurant with one-from-column-A fare. What you can find are Caribbean, Korean, Latin, Indian, and kosher Chinese restaurants springing up to serve those ethnic communities and the gastronomically curious.

Korean Chinese food is a prime example. Many Chinese migrated to Korea from the Northern provinces of China, bringing with them their use of wheat products—especially noodles. Ja jang myun is a Korean noodle dish of Chinese origin. Children, in particular, love ja jang myun, which consists of thick wheat noodles served with a special black bean sauce. The best ja jang myun noodles are made by hand and served immediately.

The Chinese dish on which ja jang myun is based is known as zha jiang mian, a specialty of northern China. Tasty and cheap to prepare, zha jiang mian has been a popular dish in northern China for centuries. If you believe the tales of Marco Polo, it may even have inspired Italian spaghetti. In any case, although considered by Koreans to be a distinctly Chinese dish, ja jang myun has taken on its own identity and tastes quite different from its Chinese equivalent. The difference lies mainly in the paste itself. Koreans have a centuries-old tradition of fermenting soybeans and appreciate great subtlety in different fermentation methods. For example, Koreans distinguish between pastes made with beans that are boiled and steamed, and those fermented in hot or mild weather. Chunjang, the Korean recipe bean paste used in ja jang

myun, balances the slightly bitter taste of fermented soybeans with a slight tinge of sweetness; for Koreans, it simply has no substitute.

Indian Chinese is rapidly gaining popularity in Queens. The hands-down favorites on an Indian-style Chinese menu are anything prepared Manchurian style (a soy-based sauce), spicy chicken "lollypops," chili chicken (or beef, pork, or shrimp), and Hakka noodles.

Cuban Chinese was one of the first overseas Chinese cuisines to debut in New York, coming during the sixties with the large influx of Cuban political refugees. Now in Queens we find more of a pan-Latino-Chinese cuisine, along with a somewhat similar Caribbean Chinese. Both are spicy and incorporate tropical ingredients.

Kosher Chinese can be summed up in on phrase: "Hold the pork." Since dairy is uncommon in Chinese cooking, the thing that differentiates kosher from other Chinese variants is the absence of pork and shellfish.

Indian Oasis
184-22 Horace Harding
Expressway, Fresh Meadows
718-353-3804
Subway: No. 7 to Main St.; Q 17
bus south to Horace Harding Exp.
Chinese and Thai food with an
Indian accent.

KOREAN CHINESE

Sam Won Gahk
82-83 Broadway, Elmhurst
718-458-0700
Subway: R to Elmhurst Ave.
For noodles with special brown
Peking sauce (ja jang myun).

Chinese Noodles and Dumplings
Flushing Mall, Booth M 38
133-31 39th Ave., Flushing
Subway 7 to Main St.
A small counter within the mall for
Chinese dumplings made for a
Korean clientele.

INDIAN CHINESE

Tangra Masala
87-09 Grand Ave., Elmhurst
718-803-2298
Subway: V, R to Grand Ave.
The original spot for Indian
Chinese continues to be a highly
popular destination.

CARIBBEAN CHINESE

The Nest
125-17 101 Ave., Richmond Hill
718-847-4035 or 4112
Subway: A to Lefferts Blvd., long
walk
West Indian and Caribbean
Chinese.

LATINO CHINESE

El Presidente Restaurant
95-49 Roosevelt Ave., Corona
718-458-4706
Subway: No. 7 to Junction Blvd.

KOSHER CHINESE

Cho-Sen Garden
64-43 108th St., Forest Hills
718-275-1300
Subway: E, F, V to 71st-
Continental Ave.

Shanghai Drunken Chicken

This popular Chinese appetizer is served cold.

INGREDIENTS

1 3-pound broiler or fryer chicken
2 slices ginger
1 green onion
2 tablespoons salt
sherry to cover chicken

DIRECTIONS

Wash and dry the chicken. Bring a large pot of water to a boil. Add the ginger, green onion, and salt, and boil for a few minutes. Add the chicken and simmer for 15 minutes. Turn off the heat and allow the chicken to cool. Drain the bird. Cut the chicken in halves, quarters, or eight pieces (two pieces for the wings, four for the legs, two for the breast and discard the back). Place the chicken pieces into a jar and cover with sherry. Keep refrigerated for several days. Before serving, cut into bite-size pieces. Garnish with cilantro if desired. Serve cold.

SERVES 4-6.

VARIATION

Save some broth from boiling the chicken and mix it with the sherry to cover the chicken.

Lion's Head Meatballs

A Shanghai casserole dish, featuring oversize pork meatballs and bok choy, traditionally cooked in a sand clay pot.

INGREDIENTS

Meatballs:

1 pound ground pork

1 slice ginger, minced

3 scallions, cut into thin slices

1 egg, lightly beaten

1 teaspoon salt (less if desired)

1 teaspoon sugar

1 tablespoon sherry

1 tablespoon light soy sauce

1/2 tablespoon cornstarch

pepper or white pepper to taste

3 tablespoons oil for cooking

1 cup chicken stock

other seasonings as desired

1 pound bok choy, washed and cut into bite-size pieces

DIRECTIONS

Place the ground pork in a bowl. Add the meatball ingredients and mix together with your hands, moving in one direction. When the ingredients are blended, wet your hands slightly and form the pork mixture into 4 large meatballs. Heat wok and add 3 tablespoons oil. Cook the meatballs on medium heat until they are golden brown. Drain the meatballs on paper towels. Heat the stock separately, adding soy sauce, sugar, and other seasonings if desired. Arrange the bok choy at the bottom of the pot and place the meatballs on top. Add the stock. Simmer until cooked (1 to 1-1/2 hours). This dish can be made in advance, frozen, and reheated.

SERVES 4-6.

Pot Stickers

INGREDIENTS

1/2 pound bok choy

3 teaspoons salt

1 pound lean ground pork

1/4 cup finely chopped green
onions, with tops

1 tablespoon Chinese cooking
wine or sweet sherry

1 teaspoon cornstarch

1 teaspoon sesame oil

dash white pepper

1 package of wonton wrappers,
cut in circles as large as
possible with a cookie cutter
or glass

1 tablespoon vegetable oil, for
cooking

1-1/2 cups chicken stock

Dipping sauce:

1/4 cup soy sauce

1 teaspoon sesame oil

1 teaspoon white vinegar

1 teaspoon hot chili oil

DIRECTIONS

Shred the bok choy into thin strips. Mix with 2 teaspoons salt and set aside
for 5 minutes. Squeeze out the excess moisture. Mix the bok choy, pork,
green onions, wine, cornstarch, the remaining teaspoon salt, sesame oil,
and pepper. Place a well-rounded teaspoonful of the mixture in the center
of a wonton wrapper. Wet edges and pinch together to encase the dough.
Repeat with the remaining slices of dough and filling.

Heat a wok or nonstick skillet until very hot. Add 1 tablespoon
vegetable oil, tilting the wok to coat the sides. Place 8 to 10 dumplings in a
single layer in the wok and fry 2 minutes, or until the bottoms are golden
brown. Add 1/2 cup chicken stock. Cover and cook 6 to 7 minutes, or until
the water is absorbed. Repeat with the remaining dumplings. Mix dipping
sauce ingredients together and serve with the pot stickers.

SERVES 6-8.

⦿ KOREAN

QUEENS IS ONE OF THE MAIN POPULATION centers for Korean immigrants to the U.S., the others being Hawaii and California. Greengroceries, which tend to fulfill the role of convenience stores in New York City, are largely owned by Koreans.

Many New Yorkers have accidentally been introduced to Korean dishes by way of salad bars that commingle Korean specialties like stuffed tofu, Korean-style sushi, and seaweed salad with the familiar salad components.

I blindly enjoyed Korean meals and snacks many times without really knowing the gestalt of Korean dining. I was fortunate to have my horizons expanded by Ishle Yi Park, the poet laureate of Queens. She was kind enough to accompany me to an excellent restaurant in the Korean part of Flushing along Northern Boulevard to teach me the ins and outs of Korean dining. I was an apt pupil.

Although there is no prescribed order for eating the many dishes served at a traditional Korean meal, many Koreans start with a small taste of soup before eating the other dishes in any order they wish. Unlike other chopstick nations, Koreans do not eat rice with chopsticks; instead they use a spoon at formal or public meals. Koreans never pick up their rice or soup bowls but leave both on the table and eat from them with spoons. Side dishes, however, are eaten with chopsticks.

At the Korean table, each person is served an individual serving of rice and soup (juk), while several side and main dishes are

FISH BREAD IS A KOREAN WAFFLE-LIKE SNACK FOOD FILLED WITH SWEET BEAN PASTE. WHEN THERE IS A STRONG RESEMBLANCE BETWEEN TWO PEOPLE, KOREANS SAY "THEY ARE FISH BREAD."

arranged for everyone to share. Though people do not need to finish all the shared food provided, it is customary to finish one's individual portion of rice. When a person leaves uneaten rice, he or she may be regarded as rude. If one is unable to eat all of one's rice, one should start with less rice. Accordingly, it is usually perfectly acceptable to ask for refills on any of the side dishes, since all traditional Korean restaurants are, in this sense, "all you can eat."

The essentials of any Korean meal are rice, soup, and panchan.

Panchan are an array of little dishes of foods flavored with sesame oil, soy sauce, ginger, and red-hot peppers that do triple duty as appetizers (you can nibble them while waiting for your meal to arrive), side dishes, and condiments. Greens—usually lettuce, Napa cabbage, or chrysanthemum leaves—are provided for wrapping around or slathering with the various panchan.

Kimchi, or fermented cabbage, is the panchan de rigueur. No Korean meal is complete without it.

It is the national food of Korea, and comes in countless variations. The favorite kimchi vegetable is Chinese (or Napa) cabbage. The Koreans ferment it in enormous quantities. They then pack the cabbage into huge earthenware jars, bury the jars in the ground up to the neck, and cover the lids with straw until the kimchi is needed.

Kimchi almost always includes hot pepper, usually dried and either ground or crushed into flakes. Because the ground, dried hot pepper sold in Korean markets is fairly mild, Koreans use generous quantities. Other common ingredients include radish, garlic, spring onion, fermented shrimp or other seafood, ginger, salt, and sugar. There are variants, including kaktugi, based on radish and containing no cabbage, and oisobagi, stuffed cucumber kimchi. Kaetnip, or sesame leaf, kimchi features layers of sesame leaves marinated in soy sauce, peppers, garlic, green onions, and other spices. Lactobacilli are heavily involved in the fermentation of kimchi, which has a higher lactic acid content than yogurt.

The formality of the meal dictates the number of panchan. The panchan might include two or three types of kimchi prepared with vegetables, meats, or seafood; grilled or steamed fish; barbecued meats; bowls of raw or slightly steamed namuls (greens or bean sprouts); and fried foods. Three is the bare minimum, even at breakfast. A Korean breakfast might consist of soup, rice, kimchi, and an array of side dishes such as tofu (tubu in Korean) or red-bean soup, with water kimchi, dried anchovies, beef strips, steamed fish, eggplant salad, or a cooked egg on top of rice gruel.

Boiled rice is the staple of Korean cuisine. Most people use sticky rice, which sometimes has beans, chestnuts, sorghum, red beans, and barley or other cereals added for flavor and nutrition. Juk is thought of as highly nutritious and light. Many varieties of juk exist, including juk made of rice, red beans, pumpkin, abalone, ginseng, pine nuts, vegetables, chicken, mushrooms, and bean sprouts.

Soup is an essential dish when rice is served. Ingredients of different soups include vegetables, meat, fish, shellfish, seaweed, and beef bones. Jjigae is similar to juk but is thicker and hardier. The most famous jjigae is made from fermented soybean paste. Jjigae is usually spicy and served piping hot in a heated stone bowl. Jeon is a kind of pancake made from mushrooms, pumpkin, slices of dried fish, oysters, unripe red peppers, meat, or other ingredients that are mixed with salt and black pepper, dipped in flour and egg, and fried in oil. Mandu are dumplings stuffed with beef, mushrooms, stir-fried zucchini, and mung bean sprouts. Pork, chicken, or fish are sometimes used instead of beef.

There are two preparations traditional to Korean cuisine that are guaranteed to please Westerners. The first is pa jon (scallion pancakes). Pa jon are eaten as a component of a large meal, as the central component of a lighter meal, or as street food. The simplest ones are cooked on a grill and made from a seasoned batter of wheat flour and glutinous rice flour, strips of sweet red and/or green pepper, and scallions. More elaborate ones may contain ground beef, oysters, clams, an assortment of vegetables, or any combination thereof.

The second is gui, signature dish of Korean cuisine, and every carnivore's favorite. Gui means "marinated meats barbecued over a charcoal fire." The most popular meats of this type, bulgogi and galbi, are marinated in soy sauce, sesame oil, garlic, and chili pepper, and cooked on a grill at the table. Many fish dishes are also cooked this way. Bulgogi literally means "fire beef." As the beef cooks, the diner takes a spoon full of rice, places a strip of the beef on the rice, adds some hot bean paste to taste, and then enfolds this inside a lettuce leaf along with some salad. Don't forget to add a few slices of the grilled garlic. The tantalizing result is something like fajitas but healthier. Definitely delicious.

DESSERT

Koreans are not big on desserts, although they do like sweet snacks. One traditional Korean dessert you might spot on a menu is sujunggwa, a refreshing chilled persimmon punch flavored with cinnamon and garnished with floating pine nuts. It is usually drunk in winter and is a healthy drink containing lots of vitamin C.

BEVERAGES

Koreans are not essentially tea drinkers like the Chinese or Japanese. Upon being seated in a Korean restaurant or home, you will likely be served a very pale-colored tea prepared from barley. This brew, which has a light, earthy flavor, is considered to be a health tea, good for one's digestive system, especially if sipped after dining.

Koreans consume more garlic per capita than any other population. I asked Ms. Park why she thought this was so. Ask a poet a question, and of course you'll get a poetic answer. She related the Korean creation myth: A god told a she-bear and a tigress that if they could exist on nothing but garlic in a cave for a hundred days, they could become human beings. The bear endured the hardship and was rewarded not only with human status but later married the god (even with what must have been monumental garlic breath). The tiger caved after very little time. The moral of this parable is about perseverance and patience eventually paying off. So eat your garlic, children.

KOREAN RESTAURANTS

Sulrak Garden Restaurant
154-01 Northern Blvd., Flushing
718-888-1850
Subway: No. 7 to Main St.
Excellent and very authentic Korean fare featuring the use of actual oak (rather than charcoal briquettes) in its tabletop barbecues. Primarily Korean clientele, but gracious to non-Koreans.

Hae Woon Dae
75-32 Broadway, Elmhurst
718-397-5834
Subway: No. 7 to Roosevelt Ave.
Generally all-around good; during peak day and evening dining times, this restaurant uses actual wood charcoal for the barbecue.

Kum Kang San Korean Restaurant and Manor
138-28 Northern Blvd., Flushing
718-461-0909
Subway: No. 7 to Main St.
This large restaurant on the site of what was once one of the most popular Chinese restaurants in Queens draws both Koreans and non-Koreans, although the Koreans are in the majority. It's a popular place for private parties, with several party rooms of various sizes and plentiful parking in back. Ask to be seated in the rear of the restaurant near the Oriental garden, if possible.

South Asia

FOR ME, INDIAN FOOD SPELLS ROMANCE.

This is because my first date with my Brit husband was for dinner at a London Indian restaurant.

I was not yet familiar with authentic Indian cuisine, and the spiciness was unanticipated, at least by me. It was back in the days when it was fashionable to wear lots of eyeliner on both the upper and lower lids. By the time we had finished our meal, I was mortified to discover long streaks of black eyeliner running down my cheeks, caused by tears in reaction to the spices. This evidently didn't put off my suitor, as our marriage has lasted for 30-plus years and still counting. My tolerance for spicy foods has gradually increased over the years so that, although I shy away from the truly incendiary, I could now easily consume the same dinner as on our first date without shedding a tear.

Indian restaurants established a beachhead in Queens during the 1970s. The catalyst was a store on 74th Street in Jackson Heights that sold luggage and electronics to Indians returning to India. The luggage store was soon joined by other businesses, notably jewelers selling 22-karat gold Indian wedding jewelry and sari shops, attracted an increasingly Indian clientele. Naturally, they had to eat somewhere, so restaurants, snack shops, and grocers were not long in following. Over the years, 74th Street has remained the nucleus of a flourishing South Asian commercial community, drawing many of its customers from distant suburbs (the residential population in the area is extremely diverse, with a Latino majority). The businesses are run, staffed, and patronized by people from all over South Asia, including Indians, Pakistanis, Bangladeshis, Nepalese, Afghanis, Sri Lankans, and Tibetans. If only relationships in that part of the world were as cooperative and harmonious as they are in Jackson Heights, where immigrants discover that their cultural similarities trump their differences in a new country.

According to census figures, between 1990 and 2000, New York's East Indian population more than doubled. Of the 170,899 Indians reported, 63 percent live in

Queens. There are burgeoning South Asian communities in eastern Queens, around Floral Park, and in Richmond Hill, which has both a large Sikh community and an Indo-Caribbean population. Unlike Jackson Heights, which draws suburbanized Indians from communities lacking South Asian goods and services, the Richmond Hill and Eastern Queens enclaves are supported largely by the local residential communities. They exist to provide desis (Hindi for paisanos) a taste of home.

Religion exerts a strong influence on diet. Strict Brahmins are usually vegetarians. Hindus who aren't vegetarians won't eat beef, in recognition of the life-supporting role of the cow. In Kashmir, Brahmins eat meat but avoid garlic and onions. Jains from the northwestern state of Gujarat follow the principle of equality for all forms of life and are not only vegetarians, they also won't consume underground roots or vegetables like onions and garlic, which are considered "passion-inducing" and a deterrent to attaining moksha—enlightenment and spiritual release from the endless cycle of reincarnation. Young leaves, tubers, and grains are also off-limits, although mature ones can be eaten. The Parsees, many of whom live in Mumbai (Bombay), consume fish, eggs, and chicken. The diet of Muslims may include mutton, goat, wild game, and beef, as long as it's halal. Pork is taboo in communities of Islamic faith but may be eaten in other religious households that are allowed to eat meat. It is illegal to slaughter a cow anywhere in the country except in heavily Christian Goa.

Each region has its own culinary intricacies. Indian cuisine ranges from simple to complex, its cooks weaving subtleties into every dish they create. Indian food can toy with your taste buds, providing you hot, bitter, sweet, tart, astringent, and nutty flavors in a single bite. It can be divided into four distinct regional styles: north, south, west, and east. Pakistan and Bangladesh, once but no longer part of India, have their own variations, but their cuisines are largely similar to those in the contiguous Indian provinces.

⊙ THE NORTH

NORTHERN INDIAN FLAVORS ARE FAMILIAR
to many Americans because they are exemplified
in the many Indian restaurants in the United
States that feature tandoori cooking.

Hindu Punjabis forced back across the border from Pakistan at the time of the partition started the first overseas Indian restaurants in 1945. With changing emigration patterns, a Punjabi-style restaurant is as likely to be operated by Pakistanis or Bangladeshis as Hindu Punjabis. A mix of Punjabi and Mughal cuisine has become the most commonly offered type of overseas Indian fare, especially at restaurants pitched to a Western clientele.

Pakistani cuisine is pretty similar to northern Indian in its spicing and sauces. The prominence of meat in Islamic Pakistan's cuisine is the most defining difference. Muslim Pakistanis don't consider a meal complete if meat is absent.

A clay-lined, bell-shaped oven, the tandoor, gives food a unique earthy aroma as well as a distinctive bright reddish-orange color to meat. The popular tandoori chicken (murgh) and doughy flat bread (naan) are probably familiar to anyone who has eaten Indian food. Kebabs, especially in Pakistani restaurants, are a delectable product of this cooking method. Stuffed breads like onion kulcha or Peshwari naan, studded with raisins, coconut, and nuts, are a sumptuous accompaniment to a meal.

Cinnamon, cloves, cardamom, fenugreek leaves, mango powder, and bay leaves are some of the herbs and spices widely used in the north. These spices are considered to have "warm" tones and are ideal for the cooler climate. Poultry and meat are more commonly included in the northern diet than elsewhere in India. Goat meat is eaten

AN INDIAN MEAL SERVED IN THE TRADITIONAL "THALI" STYLE

throughout India, but in the cooler northern regions sheep or lamb are more traditional choices. (The term mutton refers to the meat of both goat and lamb in India.) For nonmeat eaters, legumes like kidney beans, garbanzo beans, and whole black lentils provide a protein source.

The Moghuls introduced nuts, raisins, and dates. The Moghlai influence is evident in the fragrant flavors of creamy spinach sauce that drenches tender morsels of lamb, in aromatic basmati rice perfumed with saffron, whole spices, and raisins, in potatoes cooked in an almond-poppy seed sauce, and in the smoky kebabs cooked over open flames.

Balti is another cooking style with origins in the north. The name of the cooking style derives from the word for "bucket" in Urdu and Hindi, and roughly describes the two-handled wok-like

cast-iron pot used in its cooking.
Nowadays the balti cooking pot is
generally made of copper with a
steel liner, and called the karahi or
karai. A balti is usually both cooked
in the karahi and served at the
table in it. Meat and vegetables are
stir-fried along with a sauce made
from aromatic herbs and spices.

Another theory claims balti is a
bad word used to insult
unsuspecting British diners, but we
won't go there. Incidentally, when
spoken, Urdu and Hindi are almost
the same language. It is only the
written versions that differ, Hindi
being written with Sanskrit
characters and Urdu with Arabic.

Balti is now enjoyed, with good
reason, throughout Pakistan and
India, and is also very popular in
the U.K. (there are sections of
Birmingham nicknamed "the Balti
Belt"). An added advantage to
ordering a balti in a restaurant is
that, like a stir-fry, it must be
prepared fresh to order, unlike
some Indian dishes that can be
prepared in advance and reheated.

NORTHERN INDIAN/PAKISTANI RESTAURANTS

Kababish
70-64 Broadway, Jackson Heights
718-565-5131
Subway: E or F to Roosevelt Ave.,
or No. 7 to 74th St.
Take-out with great wood-fired
tandoori items like kebabs, meats,
fish, and bread.

Kababish II
34-66 74th Street, Jackson Heights
718-205-3625
Subway: E or F to Roosevelt Ave.,
or No. 7 to 74th St.
Tries to be what Kababish I isn't in
terms of a sit-down place. Many
feel that the food is better at the
original Kababish.

Ambassador 21
72-08 Broadway, Jackson Heights
718-533-7860
Subway: E or F to Roosevelt Ave.,
or No. 7 to 74th St.
Nicely decorated restaurant with
owners from the northwest frontier
of Pakistan. It offers a range of
Indian dishes, specializing in baltis.

SOUTH ASIAN PRODUCE MARKET

Fiza Diner
259-07 Hillside Ave., Floral Park
718-347-3100
Subway: F to 179th St., Q 43 Bus
to 259th St. (a shlep by public
transportation)
This modest restaurant caters
mainly to Pakistanis, Bangladeshis,
and Indian Muslims. Try its
haleem, a wheat-based dish with
lentils and spices that Bangladeshis
eat during Ramadan. Also features
karahi dishes.

Five Star Punjabi
13-15 43rd Ave. (corner 21st St.),
Long Island City
718-784-7444

Subway: E, V to 23rd and Ely
This grungy vintage diner is a long-
standing favorite of south Asian
cabbies. Good food, dismal
surroundings (although I heard
they may be renovating).

Jackson Diner
37-47 74th St, between Roosevelt
Ave. and 37th Ave., Jackson
Heights
718-672-1232
Subway: E or F to Roosevelt Ave.,
or No. 7 to 74th St.
Not a diner but a large restaurant
decorated in a vaguely retro style.
Probably the most popular Indian
restaurant in Jackson Heights

⊙ THE WEST

Mumbai is the thriving business capital of modern India. The foods here are a harmonious blend of northern and southern flavors.

Locally grown peanuts, tapioca pearls, Bishop's weed (ajwain), and cashews add to the mix, creating enhanced layers of tastes and textures. The western states have experienced India's largest migratory influences, and the food of the area reflects the combined dietary laws, food habits, and ingredients of Persian, Portuguese, Buddhist, and Jewish settlers, among others.

Sindhis are Hindus from Sind State in southwest Pakistan who migrated to Mumbai and other places in India. They retain a distinct cultural identity; and are admired for their cuisine. A lot of attention is given to how Sindhi food is prepared and what combination of dishes are best. Gujaratis, mostly vegetarian, typically eat their meals on a large, rimmed stainless steel platter called a thali, which holds a series of small bowls with several vegetable (subzi) dishes, rice, and, of

course, bread. Fried breads like rotis and puris are more common than tandoori breads. I was recently introduced to chole batura, a sensational large, puffy, fried yeast bread, much thicker than a puri, served with chick-peas. The dough is fermented slightly, giving it a faintly sourdough flavor. Dairy products like milk, buttermilk, and yogurt are staples in these parts.

Sweet and hot flavors take center stage in the west. Farther south, toward Goa, where many Portuguese settled, the European influence is apparent in the use of vinegar, as well as local treasures like cashews and coconut milk. Goan cuisine is a blend of different influences reflecting some of what the Goans had to endure over the centuries. The staple food in Goa for Hindus as well as Catholics is fish. On other fronts, however, there are vast differences between the foods of

SAMOSAS READY FOR THE FRYER

these two communities, the main reason being that the Christians also eat beef and pork, which are taboo in most Hindu households.

At this writing, I haven't spotted any Queens restaurants that can be identified as Goan, but many Indian restaurants offer vindaloos—hot, spicy dishes flavored with vinegar of Goan origin.

WESTERN RESTAURANT

Dimple Restaurant
35-68 73rd St., Jackson Heights
718-458-8144
Subway: E or F to Roosevelt Ave., or
No. 7 to 74th St.

ACCORDING TO AYURVEDIC TRADITION
Fennel is an anti-inflammatory also known for its digestive properties.

More of a snack shop than a restaurant, serving excellent Bombay-style vegetarian and sometimes Sindhi specialties.

⊙ THE SOUTH

THE FOODS OF THE SOUTH ARE NOTORIOUSLY spicy. Legumes play a prominent role in the daily diet, and rice is present in many forms in almost every dish. Bold herbs rule the thin stews, hot vegetables, and fluffy and buttery-soft rice noodles.

Cooks of the south have a knack for extracting multiple flavors from the same ingredient. A single spice, such as a mustard seed, adds different flavors to a dish, depending on whether it's used whole, dry-roasted and ground, or fried in hot oil. Coconut is another example of the disparate tastes that can be contained within a single hard shell, from its firm white flesh to the milky liquid that is made by pureeing the flesh with water. The spice blends of the south are very complex, often incorporating legumes as seasonings, a practice unheard-of in other regions of India.

Gunpowder, or milagai podi, is a condiment with a distinctly southern accent. It's made by frying lentils, chilies, and various spices together, and then grinding them into a "powder" to which additional ghee (clarified butter) is added before serving. It has a spicy/nutty flavor and a slightly granular texture that perks up rice and some of the blander dishes perfectly. Chilies, roasted mustard seed, and fresh karhi leaves are other native flavors of the south; combined with sweet, split, and hulled pigeon peas, the commingling of the flavors is disarming. Fish and seafood are bountiful staples in many nonvegetarian South Indian kitchens.

Once esoteric among Queens Indian restaurants, southern-style eateries are now proliferating. Iddli and vada are the usual starters on their menus. An iddli is a steamed

A SOUTH INDIAN DOSA SERVED WITH SAMBHAR AND CHUTNEYS

rice-and-lentil patty. A vada is a doughnut-shaped fried lentil puff. Iddli is light and fluffy and rather plain in taste and appearance, and is in need of jazzing up with sambhar and various chutneys. The vadas are served three ways: They can be had plain (mendu); soaked in rasam, a peppery tamarind-based soup (rasa vada), or chilled, soaked in yogurt, and served with sweet chutney (dahi vada).

Another southern specialty is a dosa, an Indian crêpe-like pancake, usually with a vegetable filling. Several different types of dosas and fillings are offered. Try a plain dosa or a butter dosa if you prefer mild.

The inside of the Mysore dosa is coated with hot sauce, which kicks it up more than one notch. The filling possibilities are potato, chili with cheese (paneer), and spinach with cheese. You can also choose rava dosa, made with semolina flour; unfilled paper dosa, a very thin unfilled version; Pondicherry dosa, spicy hot and unfilled; or set dosa, a set of four small unfilled ones.

Uttappam is an alternative to dosa. It resembles a large American flapjack. Instead of being filled and rolled like the dosa, it's topped, during cooking, with items like chili paneer (spiced soft cheese). (The "topping" sinks in rather than staying on top.)

All of these dishes are eaten with chutneys. Sambhar (a soupy spiced lentil and tomato sauce) is served with everything in the south. Gunpowder, mentioned earlier, and other chutneys such as the spicy green one made from green chilies, cilantro, and coconut, are usually served with southern Indian meals.

SOUTHERN INDIAN RESTAURANTS

Ganapati Temple Canteen
45-57 Bowne St., Flushing
718-460-8484; 718-460-8493
Subway: No. 7 to Main St., then Q 27 bus
This is the dining hall of a Hindu temple dedicated to Ganesh, the elephant-headed god. The intricately carved and decorated temple was disassembled in India and reconstructed in Flushing. The restaurant offers a full range of south Indian specialties. Even if the food wasn't as great as it is, the building alone would make a trip worthwhile.

Dosa Hut
45-63 Bowne St., Flushing (near 45th Avenue)
718-961-6228
Subway: No. 7 to Main St., then Q 27 bus to Holly and Bowne St.
Next door to the Hindu temple. The cuisine is southern vegetarian, the surroundings utterly without frills.

Dosa Diner
35-66 73rd St., Jackson Heights
718-205-2218
Subway: E or F to Roosevelt Ave., or No. 7 to 74th St.
A cheery vegetarian eatery for southern specialties.

Delhi Palace Indian Cuisine
37-33 74th St., Jackson Heights
718-507-0666
Subway: E or F to Roosevelt Ave., or No. 7 to 74th St.
This well-appointed sit-down eatery is not a southern-style Indian restaurant, but was one of the first to offer southern specialties like iddli and dosa in Queens. It has a full pan-Indian menu of meat and vegetarian dishes.

⊙ THE EAST

DURING INDIA'S BRITISH REGIME, THE EAST coast state of West Bengal, home of Calcutta, the most populous city in India, was India's political capital. This central location was accessible to the resort communities of Assam and Darjeeling for cool escapes from the oppressive summer heat. The soil here, drenched by the seasonal rains, and the cool climate combine to provide the ideal home for cultivating the finest teas.

The Ganges River flows into the Bay of Bengal, whose waters support hundreds of varieties of fish and shellfish. Along the coast, banana flowers flourish along with exotic vegetables and fruits like drumstick and jackfruit. In this fertile area, rice is an everyday commodity. Thanks in part to the hot and humid climate, more than 50 varieties of rice are cultivated here.

Most popular Bengali dishes are made from fish, marinated in spices or cooked in curd (which is similar to yogurt). West Bengali cuisine uses much less coconut than Bangladeshi cuisine, relying on mustard oil as a cooking medium rather than coconut oil. Its spices differ from those used in the heartland of India, but are similar to those used well inland of the east coast. The defining flavor of Bengali cooking is panchphoron, a mixture of jeera (cumin), kalonji

LET'S HAVE A CHAAT

It there was such a thing as the Ethnic Food Awards, India would blow away the competition in the snack food category. Between its street foods and its snack foods, you could happily graze your way through life on Indian munchies.

Chaats are hard to define. The word chaat literally means to lick. Chaats are a sort of Indian fast food, packed with fruits, vegetables, spices, herbs, beans or lentils, and often chicken, meat, or seafood, all seasoned with a tart, zippy, slightly sweet dressing made using chaat powder. The best chaats reflect the Indians' love of the six Ayurvedic tastes: sweet, salty, sour, salty, bitter, pungent, and stringent. The chaat powder, or chaat masala, blends multiple seasonings, including cumin, coriander, black salt, ginger, and the tart and tangy mango powder (amchoor), made from sun-dried unripe mangoes.

What would likely be street food in India shows up in Indian snack and sweet shops in Queens. These are usually unadorned self-service joints with a counter and a few tables. Try a pani poori (a puffy fried bread with chaat sauce) or a samosa chaat (a potato- and vegetable-filled pastry with chaat sauce).

(nigella), saunf (aniseed), methi (fenugreek), and rai (black mustard seed).

The east is also where India's best confectioners and sweetmeat merchants reside. Bengal's greatest contribution to the food heritage of India is a magnificent spectrum of sweets made from burnt milk and curd.

EASTERN/BANGLADESHI RESTAURANTS

Rajdhani
39-26 61st St., Woodside
718-426-7510
Subway: No. 7 to 61st-Woodside
The owner of this restaurant is Bangladeshi, and although the menu is pan-Indian, it does feature some fish and seafood offerings that reflect the Bangladeshi cooking style. Many beef dishes are on the menu, an instant giveaway that it's not Indian.

Grand Sweets & Restaurant
37-18 73rd St., Jackson Heights
718-205-4448
Subway: E or F to Roosevelt Ave.,
or No. 7 to 74th St.
Hard to find, on a little side alley
off 73rd St., but well worth the
trouble. A nice selection of eastern
and northern items. The owner is
from Bangladesh.

SAVORY MUNCHIES

When it comes to bags of stuff to
nibble on, Frito-Lay has nothing on
Indian snack foods. Snack stores
offer long lists of spiced fried
dribbles of batters, lentils, and nuts
called farsans or namkeens (salty).
Sevs are pieces of chick-pea-flour
dough pressed through a tool with
holes to form short, thin noodle
shapes and deep fried. Another
type, boondi, are formed by
pouring a thin batter through a
large perforated spatula into hot oil
to form little puffy beads. Bhel puri
is one of Bombay's favorite snacks,
a mixture of puffed rice, sev, puri,
lentils, finely chopped onions, and
chopped coriander, topped with
two kinds of chutneys: the sweet
tamarind date chutney and the
spicy onion chili chutney.

These addictive noshes are sold
in various combinations, and are

great with beer, but beware: most
westerners will drink a lot to offset
their saltiness and spiciness. Given
the use of chick-pea flour, lentils,
and nuts as components, Indian
snack foods are more protein rich
than popcorn, pretzels, and chips,
but they are deep fried, and
therefore high in fat.

DON'T SKIP DESSERT

Indian sweets are a unique pleasure
not to be missed. They are dense,
sometimes cloyingly sweet, and
sometimes laced with jarringly (to
the western palate) perfume-y or
spicy notes. Yet they are a taste
that's easy to acquire and hard to
lose. Kulfi, the Indian ice cream, is
the most universally pleasing to
western sensibilities. If you like
Häagan-Dazs, you'll probably like
kulfi. The other sweets are worth a
try for anyone with a sweet tooth.
General categories of sweets
include:

Kheer and payasa Kheer is
a rich rice pudding made out of
white basmati rice, milk, and sugar.
Payasa, a dish from southern India,
is a milk-based pudding made with
a very thin noodle called vermicelli.
Both kheer and payasa can be
flavored with saffron and
cardamom, and often include

pistachios and raisins.

Laddoos are a crumbly textured candy ball used in Hindu religious ceremonies. They are offered to gods at temples and later served as prasad (blessing from a god) to people. They are made from roasted chick-pea flour, sugar, and ghee (clarified butter). Some examples in this category include besan laddoo and motichoor laddoo.

Halva are solid puddings made of finely grated vegetables, milk, sugar, and flavorings, cut into squares. Halvas can also be grain-based, made out of semolina or even pulses like the mung bean. Some examples of popular halvas are gajar (carrot) and doodhi (squash).

Burfi are fudge-like bite-size portions of sweets made with milk or milk products, nuts, and sometimes chick-pea flour. It is commonplace for Indians to bring a box of colorful burfis as a gift to a host. Examples of some common burfis are kaju (cashew nut), badam (almond), milk Burfi, and Mysore pak (made with chick-pea flour).

Kulfi is a dense ice cream made

PAAN

Paan is made by wrapping a betel leaf around a mixture that might contain supari (betel nut), quick lime paste, karpooram (camphor), gulukand (rose petal preserve), fennel seeds, dried, grated coconut, and sometimes tobacco. The mixture varies regionally. It's consumed by placing the wad between the inside of the cheek and the teeth and holding it there as it dissolves. Paan has mild narcotic properties and stains the teeth.

In earlier times, wives offered betel leaf to their husbands to seduce them and to wean them away from other women after reciting the Vashikaran mantras 108 times. Witches are supposed to have used paan to enslave men. Dancing girls offered paan filled with intoxicants and aphrodisiacs to their clients. Thugs, in the British period, poisoned their victims by offering a cyanide-filled paan after an evening of wining, dining, dancing, and music.

Paan is sold in Jackson Heights at street stands and in some of the sweet shops.

with condensed milk and sugar and flavored with rosewater. Mango kulfi is a delicious variation. Traditionally, kulfi is set in cone-shaped molds.

Syrup-based sweets can either be milk-cheese-based or dough-based. The syrup is usually aromatic and flavored with saffron, rosewater, and cardamom. Gulab jamun is deep-fried cake. Jalebi are orange, sweet, crisp round swirls, made from plain flour and water deep-fried and then dipped in syrup.

WHAT WILL YOU HAVE TO DRINK WITH THAT?

In India, the consumption of tea as a beverage is second only to water. Called chai in India, it's brewed with water, milk, and sugar, rather than adding milk and sugar afterward. Chai masala is tea brewed with a mixture of spices as well. Indians also drink a frothy version of coffee made from coffee powder and green cardamom.

Although the natural inclination to douse the fires of highly spiced food is to drink plenty of water, it simply doesn't work. The best way to relieve the heat is with milk or a dairy-based drink. Lassi is a thin

ACCORDING TO ONE LEGEND, tea originated in India, where it grew wild in Assam and in the foothills of the Himalayas. During the Han Dynasty (A.D. 25–221), a Chinese scholar named Gan Lu went to India to study Buddhism. When he returned to China he brought back some seeds. The planting of these seeds began the cultivation of tea in China.

yogurt drink to which sweeteners, mango, or salt are often added. Plain mango juice often accompanies Indian food, but lassi is better for putting out fires. Rice and bread are also useful for counteracting an overdose of spices.

There are several very drinkable Indian beers available, most notably Kingfisher and Taj Mahal.

In Goa, a potent liqueur called feni is a highly popular drink, alone or in cocktails. There are two types: madachi (coconut) and cajuchi (cashew). In India, flights between Mumbai and Goa are nicknamed feni flights.

SWEET AND SNACK SHOPS

Rajbhog
72-27 37th Ave., between 72nd and 73rd Sts., Jackson Heights
718-458-8512
Subway: E or F to Roosevelt Ave., or No. 7 to 74th St.
and
251-21 Hillside Ave., Floral Park
718-831-1414
Subway: F to 179th St., Q43 Bus to 251st St. (a shlep by public transportation)
These two snack shops are branches of the Rajbhog Company, which makes an extensive line of Indian food products. A New Jersey branch of this outfit was a favorite of Indian filmmaker Mira Nair and actress Uma Thurman while they worked on the film *Hysterical Blindness.* Try the papri chaat.

Usha Foods and Sweets
255-03 Hillside Ave., Floral Park
718-343-1500
Subway: F to 179th St., Q43 Bus to 259th St. (A shlep by public transportation)
Great Delhi-style and South Indian vegetarian snack fare, and a wide variety of sweets and munchies. The chole bhatura (puffy sourdough bread with chick-pea

curry) rocks! Indian folks line up for their sweets around the holidays.

INDIAN GLOSSARY

Many distinct languages are spoken throughout India, so it is impossible to create a thoroughly comprehensive glossary of food terms that would comfortably fit within this chapter. The following is a collection of mainly Hindi or Urdu terms that appear frequently on Indian menus.

Murgh masala: curried chicken
Naan: flat bread made from wheat and baked in a tandoor
Namak: salt
Namkeen: salty
Paan: betel leaf stuffed with supari (betel nut), quick lime paste, kathechu paste, gulukand (rose petal preserve), fennel seeds, and dried grated coconut. Paan is usually eaten after a meal and claims to aid in digestion. Some paan connoisseurs always add tobacco to their paan. The paan is garnished with edible thin silver foil called varak.
Pakoras: popular crispy and spicy snack, usually served hot along with coriander chutney. Pakoras are a popular teatime snack served with Indian tea. Slices of

different vegetables like potatoes, onion, chilies, spinach leaves, and eggplant are dipped in a batter made out of chick-pea flour and a few dry spices, and deep-fried.

Palak, saag: spinach

Pani: water

Paneer: soft, unaged cheese, most commonly used in mutter paneer (peas and cheese) or palak (saag) paneer (spinach and cheese)

Paratha: whole-wheat unleavened flat bread, sometimes filled with cooked ground meat or a vegetable mixture. Slightly larger than a chappati and shallow fried to perfection.

Papad: thin, waferlike discs about 4 to 8 inches in diameter, made from a variety of lentils, potatoes, shrimp, rice, etc. The discs are deep-fried or dry-roasted on an open flame and served as a crispy, savory appetizer. Served in many Indian restaurants before a meal.

Pulao: delicately flavored rice, sautéed in ghee and flavored with whole spices like cumin and cloves. There are many varieties of pulao.

Puris (pooris): deep-fried whole-wheat flat breads, usually

INDIAN ETIQUETTE

Traditional Indian greetings are asalaam-o-alaykum (Muslim) or namaste (Hindu), depending on the restaurateur's origins. In India, most people eat with their fingers, believing that food doesn't taste as good when eaten with a spoon or fork. Pancakes and breads are used as eating utensils to scoop up, wrap around, or soak up food. Only the right hand is used for eating. The left hand, considered unclean, is reserved for handling a glass or spooning foods onto the plate. This can be tricky if you happen to be left-handed. I guess they don't use the expression "One hand washes the other." That being said, in America, Indians usually use cutlery, at least in public, and consider eating with one's hands déclassé or the sign of a greenhorn. Spoons are used as an all-purpose utensil, with less reliance on forks than westerners are accustomed to. Indian utensil etiquette requires that the serving spoon not touch the plate.

SOUTH ASIAN SWEETS AT SHAHEEN SWEETS IN JACKSON HEIGHTS

around 4 inches in diameter, that puff up when deep-fried and are delicious when hot

Pyaz: onion

Raan: leg of lamb marinated in yogurt-based masala

Raita: vegetable (often cucumber) and yogurt salad

Rogan josh: rich lamb curry

Roti: bread, in Hindi. Tandoori roti is bread baked in a tandoor; rumali roti, or "handkerchief bread," is a kind of a thin and flaky paratha made up of many layers.

Saag curry: aromatic curried dish made from greens

Sambhar: lentil curry from the south of India. Served as an accompaniment with iddli and dosa.

Samosas: deep-fried pastry appetizers filled with mixtures of vegetable or meat

Seekh kebab: the word seekh in Hindi means "skewer." Seekh kebab simply means kebabs on a skewer. Kebabs are usually made out of ground lamb mixed with various spices, cooked in a tandoor.

Sev: a thin, stringlike fried snack preparation made out of gram flour. Used in the preparation of sev puri and bhel Puri, or enjoyed plain. Nowadays there are many spicy and nonspicy varieties of sev available in specialty Indian stores.

Shahi: means "royal" in Hindi

Subzi: vegetable

Tandoor: the traditional Indian clay oven is the most versatile piece of equipment in the Indian kitchen. Barbecues, breads, daal, and gravies made in them acquire a unique taste, very different from food cooked in the regular oven.

Tandoori murgh: the bright red world-famous tandoori chicken, marinated with spices and yogurt, cooked in a tandoor

Thali: refers to a complete meal of several dishes of vegetables, rice, bread, chutney, and dal served on a round, rimmed stainless steel tray, also called a thali. The number and type of dishes served varies from region to region.

Tikka: skewered boneless meat cubes cooked in a tandoor

Turai: a ridge gourd, or member of the squash family

Upma: spiced semolina cooked with or without tiny cubed potatoes, peas, and sometimes shrimp, and garnished with freshly grated coconut and cilantro

Varak: fine edible silver foil used to decorate or garnish Indian desserts and paan, known to aid in digestion

Vindaloo: meat—usually pork—is used to make this very spicy and flavorful Goan dish, cooked in vinegar and typically served two to three days after it is made

Chai for Two *(and two for chai)*

INGREDIENTS

1 cup milk

1 cup water

2 teaspoons sugar, or to taste

2 teaspoons English Breakfast tea

1/4 teaspoons chai masala, or to taste

2 or 3 whole green cardamom pods

1/8 teaspoon grated fresh ginger (just a little)

DIRECTIONS

Bring milk, water, and sugar to a boil. Add remaining ingredients and allow to simmer for a minute. Remove from heat and allow to steep for 2 or 3 minutes. Strain into cups.

Mattar Paneer *(Peas with Indian cheese)*

INGREDIENTS

1 medium onion, peeled and chopped

1-inch piece of fresh ginger, peeled and chopped

1/4 cup vegetable oil

1 cup cubed paneer, plus 2 cups of the whey (see Paneec recipe)

1 whole dried red pepper

1 tablespoon ground coriander seeds

1/4 teaspoon ground turmeric

1 15-ounce can of diced tomatoes, drained

1 teaspoon salt

1/8 teaspoon freshly ground black pepper

2 packages defrosted frozen peas

DIRECTIONS

Place chopped onion and ginger into a blender or food processor along with 1/3 cup water and blend until you have a smooth paste. Leave paste in the blender container. Heat oil in a heavy 10-inch pot over a medium flame. Put the paneer into the heated oil in a single layer and fry until golden brown on all sides. Add the dried red pepper. Within 2 seconds, turn the pepper over so that it browns on both sides. With face averted, add the contents of the blender. Fry, stirring constantly, for 10-12 minutes, or until paste turns a light brown color. Add the coriander and turmeric and fry, stirring, for another minute. Add the tomatoes. Stir and fry for another 3 to 4 minutes, or until the tomatoes turn a dark reddish brown. Pour in 2 cups of the whey. Add the salt and the black pepper. Mix well and bring to a boil. Cover, lower heat, and simmer gently for 10 minutes. Lift cover and add the paneer and the peas. Cover and simmer for 10 minutes or until the peas are cooked.

SERVES 4.

Paneer *(Indian fresh cheese)*

INGREDIENTS
½ gallon whole milk
⅛ cup (1 ounce) white vinegar
vegetable oil for deep-frying

DIRECTIONS
Heat milk to boiling over medium-high heat, stirring frequently to prevent scorching. Stir in vinegar; remove from heat. The milk will immediately separate into curds (solids) and whey (liquid). Line large colander with cheesecloth or muslin; place over bowl. Pour curds and whey mixture into lined colander. Reserve the whey collected in the bowl for above recipe. Lift edges of cloth; swirl in sink once or twice to remove excess liquid. Completely wrap curds in cloth; return to colander. Place a large jar, Dutch oven, or stockpot filled with water or similar weight directly on curds. Leave undisturbed in sink 5 to 6 hours to drain. Remove weight and remove cheese to cutting board; discard cheesecloth. Cut cheese into ¹/₂-inch cubes. Cover and refrigerate at least 2 hours or up to 12 hours.

Kheer *(Indian rice pudding)*

INGREDIENTS

1/2 cup short-grain or pearl rice
8 almonds, blanched
8 pistachios
8-10 threads saffron
2 teaspoons hot milk
1 quart whole milk
1/2 cup sugar
1/4 teaspoon cardamom powder

DIRECTIONS

Wash rice and soak it in plenty of water for 20 minutes. Drain. Coarsely chop the nuts. Dissolve saffron by rubbing it in hot milk. Heat half the whole milk, add the rice, and stir till it boils. Reduce heat, allowing rice to cook in the milk until it's almost done. Add the remaining milk, sugar, cardamom, saffron, and nuts. Bring back to a boil, stirring gently but continuously. Reduce heat. Simmer for 2-3 minutes. Serve hot or chilled.

SERVES 6.

Southeast Asia

SOUTHEAST ASIA HAS A POPULATION OF 550 million and an area of 1.6 million square miles, extending from Myanmar to the Philippines, including the Indochinese and Malay peninsulas and adjacent archipelagos.

The region's cuisines are influenced by China to the north and India to the west. Southeast Asia includes the countries of Brunei, Myanmar (formerly known as Burma), Cambodia (Kampuchea), Indonesia, Laos, Malaysia, the Philippines, Singapore, Thailand, and Vietnam.

According to the 2000 census, Southeast Asians represent only the tiniest blip in Queens's population of 2,229,379. Filipinos are in the lead at 30,520, or 1.4 percent of the population. Next come the Vietnamese with 3,268, or 0.1 percent. Countries like Thailand, Indonesia, and Malaysia are lumped together in a category of "other Asian," weighing in at 35,041, or 1.6 percent of Queens residents. Assuming these numbers are correct, then Queens's Southeast Asian communities are a

IN SOUTHEAST ASIA MEALS are not served in courses. All foods arrive at the table together. In Thailand, people eat with a spoon and fork. In Indonesia and Malaysia, people eat with their (right) hands, and spoons are used for serving. Vietnam is the only country in this region that uses chopsticks.

bunch of overachievers, culinarily speaking. The significant contributions of countries like Thailand, Malaysia, and Indonesia, as measured on my Queens Yumminess Scale, belies these figures.

⊙ THE PHILIPPINES

QUEENS'S LITTLE MANILA IS A CLUSTER OF businesses at the intersection of Roosevelt Avenue and 70th Street. There are four restaurants, a couple of deli/markets, and other businesses run by and for Filipinos.

Ihawan is a restaurant one flight above a take-out place that bills itself as "home of the best barbecue in town." That's a pretty big claim, especially if you take into account the mind-boggling variety of styles of ethnic barbecues available in Queens from places like China, Central Asia, India, the Caribbean, and South America. Still, if you regard barbecue from a strictly Filipino perspective, I can imagine arriving at that conclusion.

Ihawan offers a broad range of Filipino dishes, reflecting the varied influences on its cuisine. In fact, it offers such a variety of pig parts that it received the dubious distinction on the *Village Voice*'s "Best of NYC" list of having the "Most Extensive Organ Meat Selection." Pork ears, anyone?

The Philippines is yet another country where history and geography conspire to shape gastronomic destiny. Dishes are a mix of Malay, Spanish, Chinese, Japanese, and American flavors. For example, the use of coconut milk as an ingredient originated in Malaysia. Lumpia or lumpiang Shanghai (similar to spring rolls) and pancit (noodles mixed with pork, shrimp, and vegetables) are Chinese in origin. Several Filipino traditional dishes retain Spanish names, like mechado (beef with pork fat), menudo (diced meat and potatoes stewed in tomato sauce), and pochero (a blend of pork, cabbage, green beans, and other vegetables). The American contribution to the

Filipino kitchen came after World War II, when surplus canned foods became widely available and fresh foods were in short supply. The Filipinos embraced these new foods and turned them into dishes that taste nothing like canned food. For example, by sautéing canned corned beef with onions and garlic, they created a dish uniquely their own.

For most Filipinos, a meal is never complete without rice. In fact, the Filipino word for rice, kanin, is related to the Filipino verb kain, meaning "to eat." Unlike English speakers, which call all forms "rice," Filipinos have a lot of terms for rice: palay for rice that is harvested but not cleaned, bigas for the uncooked rice grains, sinaing for rice that is still cooking in a pot, and kanin for the cooked rice, among others. Many Filipino desserts are also made from rice, and are generally called kakanin.

Early Filipinos cooked their food minimally by roasting, steaming, or boiling. The freshest of fish was made into kinilaw, "cooked" by immersion in vinegar and salt with ginger, onions, and red peppers—a dish similar to the Latin American ceviche.

Sour, salty flavors are preferred by Filipinos. Unripe fruits like tamarind, mango, and guava provide sour power, as well as the tiny kalamansi, a citrus halfway between an orange and a lime, which is sour even when ripe. For salty flavoring, Filipinos rely on patis or fish sauce, bagoong or shrimp paste, and, with the arrival of the Chinese, soy sauce. Lumpia, the Filipino version of spring rolls, are served with a simple dipping sauce of crushed garlic and vinegar.

Adobo, the national dish of the Philippines, bespeaks Spanish influence. In Mexico, adobo is a marinade and condiment. In the Philippines, it is a dish of well-marinated braised chicken and pork with coconut milk, utilizing many of the same condiments as the similarly named Mexican sauce.

These are some of the other famous and delicious dishes to look for at a Filipino eatery:

Inihaw na talong is broiled eggplant with chopped tomato, onions, and bagoong.

Kare-kare is a meaty oxtail stew with pieces of tripe and vegetables in peanut sauce.

Lumpia comes either fresh (lumpiang sariwa) or fried (fried lumpia, lumpiang Shanghai). Lumpiang sariwa are like crepes (rice/egg pastry) filled with Chinese vegetables and topped with peanut sauce, while the Shanghais are small spring rolls of rice pastry filled with ground beef or pork. Fried lumpias are basically the fresh variety deep-fried to perfection.

Pancit is a mound of sautéed noodles laced with bits of fresh vegetables, thinly sliced savory sausage, and tiny shrimps. Different types of noodles can be used: bihon (rice noodles), canton (flour noodles), sotanghon (soybean noodles), and mike (pronounced as mee-kee, fresh egg noodles).

Rellenong manok is a whole chicken, deboned and stuffed with a mixture of ground chicken, pork, and ham, plus whole sausages and hard-boiled eggs, so that when it is served, the slices look as decorative as they are tasty.

Tinolang tahong is a soup made with mussels steamed in gingerroot, spinach, and a bit of onion.

DESSERTS

The signature dessert of the Philippines is halo halo, a sort of tropical answer to the English trifle. Literally meaning "mix mix," it is made from a combination of tropical fruits, sweetened beans, shaved ice, and macapuno (a Philippine variety of the coconut, also called "sport coconut," the meat of which is soft and jelly-like),

topped with whipped or ice cream and served in a tall glass. Also look for leche flan and brazos, which are custards wrapped in meringue.

BEVERAGES

Beer is very popular with Filipinos, especially their own San Miguel. They also make a rum called Tanduay. In the Philippines, there are many indigenous drinks that are seldom exported. Tuba (coconut toddy) is common in coconut-growing areas. Tuba is made through the process of extracting the sap of an unopened coconut bud. The fresh sap is sweet and nonalcoholic. Allowed to ferment, tuba has a stinging sweet and bittersweet taste and is sometimes dyed with mangrove bark. Tuba can also be made from the sap of buri and nipa palms. It's known locally as "jungle wine."

Tuba can be distilled to lambanog, a potent liquor. Lambanog is a local moonshine, as it is surreptitiously distilled in hidden stills, a process that makes it as prized a possession as a vintage wine. The Ybanag of the Cagayan Valley make layaw, a very strong corn spirit. In the mountain provinces of northern Luzon, rice is fermented to form tapuy (rice wine). The Kalingas and Ilocanos are noted for basi, a sugarcane wine.

Filipinos are no slouches when it comes to fruit drinks, either. Sago at gutaman is a sweet drink mixed with pearl tapioca and gelatin, somewhat reminiscent of bubble tea. Iced buko is young coconut juice over ice full of large flakes of coconut. Melon is a sweet liquid cantaloupe over ice with shredded cantaloupe within. In season there is iced kalamansi, that sour citrus fruit favored by Filipinos, sweetened and served over ice.

FILIPINO RESTAURANTS

A popular style of Filipino restaurant is called turo-turo. Turo-turo is derived from the Tagalog verb turo, meaning "to point." Turo-turo is a slang expression for fast-food restaurants where customers point to the dish they want to order. Trying turo-turo is a quick and easy way to taste your way through a wonderful variety of dishes. Most of the following restaurants offer turo-turo. Filipino restaurants tend to close by 8 p.m., sometimes earlier, so plan your meal accordingly.

Krystal's Cafe / Stasi Pastry Shop
69-02 Roosevelt Ave., Woodside
718-426-8676
Subway: E or F to Roosevelt Ave., Jackson Heights, or No. 7 to 74th St.

This place has a small cafe downstairs and a large dining room upstairs. It offers both table service and a lunch buffet. A large selection of pastries are featured behind the counter.

Ihawan
40-06 70th St. (on the corner of 69-09 Roosevelt Ave., upstairs), Woodside
718-205-1480
Subway: E or F to Roosevelt Ave., Jackson Heights, or No. 7 to 74th St.
Self-proclaimed "home of the best barbecue in town." You can buy uncooked food here to bring home, or stay and eat in the upstairs dining room.

Perlas ng Silangan
69-09 Roosevelt Ave., Woodside
718-779-2991
Subway: E or F to Roosevelt Ave., Jackson Heights, or No. to 74th St.
A large restaurant space with table service.

Renee's Kitchenette Filipino
69-14 Roosevelt Ave., Woodside
718-476-9002
Subway: E or F to Roosevelt Ave., Jackson Heights, or No. 7 to 74th St.
Tiny. Cheap enough to taste everything.

Pancit Bihon

INGREDIENTS

1 3-lb. chicken that's been
boiled with 1 onion, 2 celery
stalks, and 4 peppercorns
until falling off bones,
reserving stock

stock reserved from chicken

oil for frying

2 cloves garlic, crushed

1 medium onion, sliced

1 lb. pork, sliced into thin strips

patis (Filipino fish sauce) to taste

ground black pepper

1 cup medium shrimp, cooked,
shelled, and deveined

1 can straw mushrooms

1 small carrot, julienned

1 can water chestnuts

1/2 head of bok choy (pechay) or 1/2
head cabbage, julienned

a few snow pea pods

1/2 lb. mussels or scallops (optional)

1 or 2 packages of pancit canton, or
a package of vermicelli or angel
hair pasta

salt

4 or 5 green onions

1 lemon

DIRECTIONS

Remove boiled chicken from bones and discard bones, reserving stock.
Heat oil in a pan (or wok if possible). Sauté garlic and onion until the
onion is transparent. Add chicken and pork. Cook until pork is brown. Add
half the chicken stock. Boil for about 3 minutes. Add patis to taste.
Sprinkle on ground black pepper. Simmer for about another three minutes.
Add shrimp, mushrooms, carrots, and other ingredients except for the
noodles, green onions, lemon, and salt. Simmer, covered, for another 3
minutes or so. Add the remaining stock. Adjust the taste with salt, pepper,
and patis. Add the noodles. Mix thoroughly until noodles are soft. Garnish
with sliced green onions and sliced lemon. Serve with lemon juice.

SERVES 6-8.

Halo Halo

INGREDIENTS

4 cups ice shavings

4 tablespoons sweet adzuki
beans

4 tablespoons macapuno
(coconut sport)

4 tablespoons diced preserved
jackfruit

4 tablespoons preserved sugar
palm

4 tablespoons diced kiwi

4 tablespoons diced strawberries

½ pint heavy cream, whipped
(or use Redi-Whip)

DIRECTIONS

Fill four glasses with the ice shavings. Place rest of the ingredients on top of
the ice. Top generously with whipped cream.

SERVES 4.

⦿ VIETNAM

VIETNAMESE PEOPLE SHOW UP ON THE 2000 census as 1 percent (3,268) of the population of Queens. They have no clearly identifiable community, but enough restaurants to make their cuisine worthy of mention.

Vietnamese cooking is generally regarded as the lightest of the Southeast Asian cuisines. It retains a bit of a French accent as its legacy of colonial times. The Vietnamese don't play as fast and loose with coconut milk and other rich ingredients, nor is their food painfully spicy. Stir-frying plays a relatively minor role in Vietnamese cuisine, and once again is seen more in the north than elsewhere. Frying in general is less important than simmering. Fish and seafood are central to the Vietnamese diet. Meats are also common, but in smaller quantities relative to vegetables and noodles. Vegetables are often left raw, especially in the south, to act as a fresh contrast to the spicy cooked meat.

Soy sauce rarely appears in Vietnamese dishes except in the north. It is replaced by what is perhaps the most dominant ingredient in all of Vietnamese cuisine—nuoc mam, or fish sauce. The prevailing flavors of Vietnamese food come from mint leaves, coriander, lemongrass, shrimp, nuoc mam, star anise, ginger, black pepper, garlic, basil, rice vinegar, sugar, and green onions. Many flavorful marinades are made by some combination of these flavorings. Marinated meat or fish is quickly sautéed in the wok and served with an array of raw vegetables and herbs. All this may be eaten over rice or rolled in a rice-paper wrapper or lettuce leaf (or both), then dipped into a pungent sauce. Usually served as an appetizer here, this is an example of nhau (little bites) served fresh from the grill as finger foods. The favorite dipping sauce is nuoc cham, made from fish sauce, water, sugar, and lime juice and seasoned with chilies and garlic.

Like other Asian people, the Vietnamese eat a lot of rice. But noodles are really the backbone of this cuisine. Noodles are eaten wet and dry, in soup or with soup, and are made in different shapes and thicknesses from wheat, rice, and mung beans.

No Vietnamese meal is complete without fresh vegetables and herbs. A platter of cucumbers, bean threads, slices of hot pepper, and sprigs of basil, coriander, mint, and a number of related herbs found principally in Southeast Asia is obligatory at every meal.

Pho (pronounced "fuh") is the national dish of Vietnam. Picture large bowls of steaming hot soup with rice or wheat-based noodles, contrasting fresh, cold herbs, bean sprouts, pieces of pork, chicken, or beef, and bits of tangy, preserved cabbage.

A creation from Hanoi, pho has been around for only about 100 years, the blink of an eye in Asian calculation of time. Originally pho was just boiled beef, noodles, and broth. Creative cooks then developed the raw beef version (pho bo tai) and chicken pho (pho ga), and during wartime, when beef was scarce, they made pork pho (pho lon). Though countless regional variations exist, pho is generally associated with beef.

Garnishes and condiments are a big part of the enjoyment of pho. Some of the popular ones include raw or blanched bean sprouts; chilies; Vietnamese herbs like ngo gai (cilantro, thorny cilantro, saw-leaf herb), Thai basil (hung que), and spearmint (hung lui); a squeeze of lime; and hoisin (tuong) or Sriracha hot sauce.

The Vietnamese are as likely to eat pho for breakfast as they are for any other meal of the day, which is pretty likely.

The French connection is evident in the popular Vietnamese sandwiches, bán mi. These are toothsome "heros" of garlicky meats, pickled daikon, carrot, chilies, cucumber, and cilantro, built on a baguette sauced with mayo and soy sauce. What's not to like?

DESSERTS

Desserts are not an important part of Vietnamese cuisine, although many Vietnamese cooks are also accomplished French pastry chefs. There are usually a limited number of dessert options on Vietnamese restaurant menus, but don't count on them to be a high point of your meal. Expect a few varieties of puddings made from rice, or tapioca starch and pearls, or flan. Moon cakes—pastries stuffed with sweet lotus seeds or red beans—are eaten as snacks, especially during celebrations.

BEVERAGES

Vietnamese drink a variety of soft drinks, teas, French-style and rice wines, and a lot of coffee, all served in a uniquely Vietnamese manner. You might find soda sua hot ga (soda with egg yolk and condensed milk), or soda xi muoi (salty plum soda).

Vietnam is one of the largest coffee producers in the world. The Vietnamese drink very strong espresso-like coffee prepared in a one-serving metal coffee press. A small, straight-sided glass cup is filled about one-third full with sweetened condensed milk. The coffee press is held over the cup as the coffee is prepared. Properly prepared Vietnamese coffee should resemble a monochromatic brown rainbow in the cup. Coffee made in this manner, and then served over ice, is also very popular. Vietnamese coffee made the traditional way seems to be gaining ground as the latest trendy way to enjoy coffee.

VIETNAMESE RESTAURANTS

Pho Bang Restaurant
82-90 Broadway, Elmhurst
718-205-1500
Subway: G, R, or V to Elmhurst Ave.
and
41-07 Kissena Blvd., Flushing
718-939-5520
Subway: No. 7 to Main Street
These authentic Vietnamese restaurants are part of a chain with branches in several other cities throughout the United States.

Pho Bac
82-78 Broadway, Elmhurst
718-639-0000
Subway: G, R, or V to Elmhurst Ave.
Emphasis is on seafood here.

Pho Vietnamese Restaurant
38-02 Prince St., Flushing
718-461-8686
Subway: No. 7 to Main Street

Pho *(adapted to American ingredients)*

INGREDIENTS

Soup:

4 quarts beef broth (canned
   unless you're really ambitious)

2 large onions, thinly sliced

6 slices of fresh ginger

1 cinnamon stick

1 star anise

1 teaspoon whole black
   peppercorns

2 cloves garlic, peeled and
   smashed

Optional garnish ingredients:

1 cup loosely packed fresh basil
   leaves

1 cup loosely packed fresh mint
   sprigs

1 cup loosely packed cilantro sprigs

3 fresh jalapeño peppers, thinly
   sliced

2-3 lime wedges

hoisin sauce

hot pepper sauce

Vietnamese fish sauce (nuoc mam)

1 pound sirloin tip, thinly sliced
   (for easier slicing, chill in freezer
   20 minutes before slicing)

2 8-oz. packages dried rice
   noodles

DIRECTIONS

In a large stockpot add broth, onions, ginger, cinnamon, star anise, peppercorns, and garlic. Bring to a boil, then reduce heat to low and cover. Simmer for 1 hour, stirring occasionally. Arrange garnish ingredients onto separate plates and bowls at the table. Soak rice noodles in hot water (do not boil) for 15 minutes or until softened; drain (do not rinse with cold water). Place equal amounts of noodles in soup bowls and cover with raw beef slices. Ladle hot broth over noodles and beef (the beef slices should cook or brown in the hot broth). Garnish to taste.

SERVES 6-8.

Café sua nong *(Vietnamese coffee)*

INGREDIENTS

2-4 tablespoons sweetened condensed milk

6 oz. hot coffee made from Vietnamese (or espresso or dark French roast) beans

DIRECTIONS

Place the milk in the bottom of an 8-ounce glass. Carefully pour in coffee, trying not to disturb the layer of milk. Stir milk up from bottom and sip coffee.

VARIATION

Café sua da. Add ice cubes on top of the sweet milk and proceed as above. Serve iced.

SERVES 1.

⊙ THAILAND

WHY DID THE CENSUS BUREAU LUMP THE
Thai community into "other Asian"? Weren't they
paying attention? Even I know of two Thai
Buddhist temples: New York Dhammaram Temple,
33-37 97th St., Corona, and Wat Budda Thai, 76-
16 46th Ave., Elmhurst. Somebody is supporting
them, and I don't think it's the Albanians.

There are Thai food stores on Broadway in Elmhurst, and at least two bagel bakeries under Thai ownership, serving Thai food on the side. That's not counting the numerous Thai restaurants around the borough, some catering primarily to Thais and others to westerners. Less than 1 percent of Queens's population, not meriting their own category? As we say in Queens, get OUT!

Thai cuisine, almost unknown 15 years ago, has taken American palates by storm. It is one of the big success stories of recent immigrants' ethnic food. Still, while many Americans have sampled and enjoyed Thai fare, it is still new enough to our collective culinary vocabulary to be worthy of further illumination. Besides, Queens is one of the few localities where you can enjoy Thai cuisine prepared for the sensibilities of ethnic Thais, rather than a modified version meant to please western palates.

A great Thai meal can be a religious experience for those of us who find our salvation in wonderful food. Thai foods have strong, hot flavors marked by a wide range of tastes, textures, temperatures, and colors, which are balanced to provide

THAI BUDDHIST MONKS AT WAT BUDDHA THAI TRAVORNVANANAM OF NEW YORK IN ELMHURST. THE TEMPLE DOES AN ANNUAL SONGKRAN (THAI NEW YEAR) CELEBRATION WITH FOOD AND TRADITIONAL MUSIC AND DANCE WHICH THE PUBLIC MAY ATTEND. CALL FOR DETAILS **718-803-9881.**

variety and harmony in a meal. An ideal Thai meal balances spicy, sour, salty, sweet, bitter, and hot, while also pleasing the palate, nose, and eye.

Thailand has never been conquered or colonized (something that can't be said of many countries), and its food is unique. Its neighbors, India and China, have both influenced Thailand's cuisine, yet Thailand's food, like her people, has maintained its own distinct identity.

Fish is a staple of the Thai diet. Fish sauce (nam pla) and/or shrimp paste (kapee) appear in nearly every recipe. The chile has become a

central player, and much Thai food is fiery hot. The other distinct flavors of Thai cooking come from indigenous spices and produce: lemongrass, tamarind, ginger, black pepper, galangal, garlic, cilantro, basil, palm sugar, turmeric, cumin, shallots, and green onions. Peanuts and coconut are frequently used in Thai curries as well.

Rice—mostly steamed long-grain jasmine rice with a delicate natural perfume—is central to the Thai meal. It is cooked without salt to balance the salty flavors in accompanying dishes, served so if you choose a Thai restaurant that caters to its nationals, come prepared for incendiary spices. Toning down the heat often destroys the balance of flavors, and the dish just isn't the same. As relief, eat plenty of rice and drink some beer; tempting as it is, water doesn't help.

steaming hot, and kept at the desired temperature in a covered container or individual woven baskets. It is perfectly acceptable to eat this rice with your fingers, tearing off chunks and dipping them in whatever appeals to you before popping it into your mouth.

A Thai meal, traditionally eaten with a spoon, consists of white rice with a variety of accompaniments — a curry, stir-fry, grilled, fried, or steamed dish, a spicy hot-and-sour salad or vegetable dish, and soup. Sometimes different flavors are presented in a single dish, as in a bowl meal, or through many side dishes and condiments. Soup and salad are eaten either at the beginning or end of a meal. Salads

are fiery, aromatic, and crispy, with grilled meat or chicken, fresh fruit or vegetables, chile peppers, and leafy spices. Tidbits or appetizers called khong wang also sometimes become part of a meal.

For breakfast, Thais usually eat khao thom, rice porridge that has a pleasant vinegary taste, with herbs, onion, and garlic, served as a hot dish, often with an egg mixed in. Or they eat jok, which is similar to khao thom but thicker and more bland, and also served as a hot dish.

Lunches are usually a one-dish meal. One-dish or bowl meals are also popular as snacks and quick-to-fix dinners. Based on rice or noodles with meat, chicken or seafood, and vegetables, these meals tend to be spicy, and are frequently accompanied by condiments and garnishes.

Paad Thai, a stir-fried rice noodle dish with meat and vegetables, can be considered Thailand's national dish, and is found in virtually every Thai restaurant. Tom yam kung, shrimp and straw mushrooms in a hot, spicy, and sour soup, is almost on a par with paad Thai in terms of popularity.

Many different Thai curries are served. Some of the best known are gaeng Mussaman (Muslim curry), gaeng phanaeng, gaeng phet, and gaeng liang. The most popular among Thais is gaeng pet. (Gaeng is pronounced like the English word gang and means "curry"; pet means "spicy hot.") The basic ingredients (khreuang gaeng) in gaeng pet are red chili, peppercorn, garlic, salt, shallots (small red onions), coriander root, lemongrass, kaffir lime rind and leaves, krachai (boesenbergia pandurata), galanga (languas galanga), and kakpi (Thai shrimp paste).

Coconut and its milk are ingredients the Thai have in common with other Southeast Asian and Pacific cuisines. Coconut milk blends and mellows the flavors of the dishes in which it is used. As a liquid medium in meat and fish curries, it offsets the pungency of many of the stronger ingredients. Coconut is the dairy product substitute of Southeast Asia.

DESSERTS

After a Thai meal, you are probably craving something cold and sweet to cool down your mouth. Dessert at Thai restaurants can either be simple or elaborate. Coconut ice cream and various tropical fruit-infused sorbets or sherbets can be found on most menus. Fried bananas are also common. Also look for look choop, Thailand's answer to marzipan. These adorably realistic little fruits and vegetables, fashioned of sweet bean paste, have a sweet coconutty mellow flavor. Sripraphai, listed below, has 'em.

BEVERAGES

Thais have their own take on iced and hot coffee and iced tea, all made from extra-strong brews and mellowed with sweetened condensed milk. Singha is the Thai brand of beer. Beer goes down easily with spicy hot Thai food. As in all tropical countries, fruit juices and drinks are also popular.

HERE ARE A FEW TERMS WILL HELP YOU NAVIGATE A THAI MENU

tom (soup), yum (salad), khao (rice), mee (noodles), kaeng phed (hot soup or curry), kaeng chud (mild soup or curry), nam prik (hot dipping sauce), nam oi (sweet sauce), pla (fish), poo (crab), goong (prawns), nuer (beef), and moo (pork—do pigs moo in Thailand?).

THAI RESTAURANTS

Sripraphai
64-13 39th Ave., Woodside
718-899-9599
Subway: No. 7 to 61st St.
This restaurant is the darling of the
foodies, not without good reason. Its
food is authentic, delicious, and
reasonably priced. As of this writing,
it was expanding its modest quarters.

Arharn Thai
32-05 36th Ave. (between 32nd &
33rd streets), Astoria
718-728-5563
Subway: N or W to 36th Ave.
Great food, modest prices.

Zabb
71-28 Roosevelt Ave., Elmhurst
718-426-7992
Subway: E or F to Roosevelt Ave.,
Jackson Heights, or No. 7 to 74th St.
Zabb specializes in Esan (Isan, Isaan)
Thai, the cuisine of northeastern
Thailand. Try its jaow esan soup, the
Thai version of hot pot.

Arunee Thai Cuisine
37-68 79th St. between Roosevelt &
37th Aves., Jackson Heights
718-205-5559
Subway: No. 7 to 82nd St.
They like to turn up the heat here,
but don't charge extra for it. Quite
authentic. Cheap.

Erawan
42-31 Bell Blvd. between 43rd Ave.
& Northern Blvd., Bayside
718-428-2112
Subway: No. 7 to Main St., then Q
13 to Northern Blvd. Or take the
LIRR to Bayside Station
More upscale both in ambience and
price than any of the previous ones,
this Thai eatery caters more to
gringos. If you can't stand the heat,
try this kitchen.

Rice Avenue
72-19 Roosevelt Ave., Jackson
Heights
718-803-9001
Subway: E or F to Roosevelt Ave.,
Jackson Heights, or No. 7 to 74th St.
Feels upscale until you get the check;
Rice Avenue supplies the ambience
gratis. Good food, modest prices.

Ubol's Kitchen
24-42 Steinway St., Astoria
718-545-2874
Subway: N or W to Astoria Blvd.
An old-timer as Queens Thai goes,
this restaurant is nestled in the heart
of Little Egypt. Dependable Thai
fare.

Pad Thai

INGREDIENTS

1 pack dried rice stick noodles
 or sen lek

1/4 cup vegetable oil

2 tablespoons smashed garlic

2 tablespoons smashed onion

1/2 cup pressed bean curd, cut
 into small strips

1/2 cup dried shrimp

1/2 cup roasted unsalted peanuts
 made into a paste with a mortar
 and pestle or food processor

1/2 cup fish sauce (nam pla)

1/2 cup soy sauce

1/4 cup sugar

2 teaspoons pepper powder

1 pound chicken meat cut into
 small bite-size pieces

6 eggs

1/2 cup of water

1 cup fresh bean sprouts, washed

1/2 cup chives cut into 1-inch pieces

DIRECTIONS

Soak the rice stick noodles in tepid water for roughly 15 minutes. Then cut the noodles into 4-inch pieces. Strain the noodles and set them aside. Using a wok (or large skillet), with burner turned up as high as possible, heat the vegetable oil and add the garlic, onion and tofu. Stir for 2 minutes. Add the dried shrimp and stir. Then, one at a time, add in the peanuts, fish sauce, soy sauce, sugar, pepper, and chicken, stirring the mixture the entire time. Make sure the chicken has cooked (turned white) before proceeding to the next step. Add the eggs and continue to stir the mixture. Add in 1/2 cup of water. Add the noodles, and be sure to stir! The noodles tend to burn if not continuously stirred. Check to see if the taste of the dish is suitable to you; if not, add in either fish sauce (salty), sugar (sweet), or soy sauce (salty), depending on your preference. The final step is to add in the bean sprouts and chives, just before turning off the burner.

Pad Thai is normally garnished with a heaping portion of uncooked bean sprouts on the side and a sprig of cilantro on top.

SERVES 2-3 AS A ONE-DISH MEAL.

Laab gai *(Thai chicken salad)*

INGREDIENTS

2 pounds ground chicken

2 tablespoons peanut oil

fish sauce (nam pla) to taste

4 tablespoons lemon juice

1/2 cup green onion (sliced)

1/2 cup red onion cut into thin wedges

1 teaspoon prik Thai on (young green peppercorns, usually still
    attached to their stem), chopped

1/2 cup mint leaves (shredded)

1 cup ground, roasted rice*

DIRECTIONS

Heat oil in a large wok or skillet. Stir-fry the chicken until it completely loses its pink color. Allow to cool. Mix the chicken with fish sauce and then add lemon juice. Add green onion, red onion, pepper, and mint leaves. Add more fish sauce or lemon juice to taste. Add the roasted rice powder. Correct ingredients to taste. Serve with rice or sticky rice, and lettuce leaves to eat it with.

SERVES 6-8.

*Note: To prepare the ground roasted rice, heat a pan and put in 1 cup of rice, stirring it back and forth until it browns. After it cools, grind it in a coffee grinder or food processor. If you cannot find fresh prik Thai, use 1/2 tsp. of dried; you'll have to roast it first and then grind it.

⊙ ASIAN: MALAYSIA AND INDONESIA

INFORMATION ON THE REMAINING "other Asian" immigrant communities in Queens is sketchy at best. They have no obvious clusters of businesses or noticeable cultural institutions. Nonetheless, it is our good fortune that at least two of these countries, Malaysia and Indonesia, have left their gastronomic mark on the borough.

Malaysian cuisine seems to be growing in popularity, and may be poised to become the next ethnic cuisine to go mainstream. The giveaway is that like Thai restaurants, Malaysian eateries are popping up in very un-Asian neighborhoods. Some Thai restaurants are also billing themselves as Thai-Malaysian. With foodies always hungry for the next new thing, can Indonesian be far behind?

The cuisines of Malaysia and Indonesia have a lot in common.

Both are intricate and varied. Both are predominantly Muslim countries that shy away from pork, eat a lot of seafood, enhance their sauces with coconut milk, and have evolved with many of the same culinary influences. Rice is the main staple, although both consume plenty of noodles.

Malaysian food is actually an amalgamation of influences originating from its multiethnic population of Malay, Indian, Eurasian, Chinese, Nyonya (pronounced nyah nyah), and the indigenous peoples of Borneo. In most Malaysian dishes, one influence predominates, but is usually tempered by the others. It would be fair to say that most Malaysian fare tends to be spicy (but not painfully so) and sweet in varying degrees, with hints of coconut and slightly fishy undertones. By the way, if you have a cholesterol problem, this may not be your optimal cuisine. It relies heavily on the use of coconut milk, coconut oil, and palm oil. Even if you avoid the fried dishes (which abound), the sauces are laced with the aforementioned ingredients and the meats are fatty.

Indonesia's culinary ties are closest to those Southeast Asian countries strongly influenced by India. Indonesian food combines influences from India, the Middle East, China, and Europe. There are also the New World products brought by Spanish and Portuguese traders long before the Dutch colonized the islands.

The Queens Indonesian restaurants serve Padang-style food. Sumatra has a number of local styles of cooking, but the most famous is masakan Padang, the burning-hot cuisine of the Minangkabau of Western Sumatra, named after the provincial capital of Padang.

Three dishes that Malaysia and Indonesia have in common are satay (sate), redang, and nasi goreng. Satay, marinated barbecued beef, chicken, or lamb on wooden skewers served with peanut sauce, is a popular appetizer and snack food in both countries. Redang (rending) is a slow-cooked meat stew made with coconut milk and spices. Nasi goreng is fried rice with bits of meat, shrimp, egg, and vegetables.

HERE ARE SOME MALAYSIAN FAVES

Nasi lemak is a rice dish cooked in coconut milk. It's served with ikan bilis (anchovies), sambal, boiled egg, fried peanuts, and cucumber slices. This is also a popular breakfast dish.

Roti canai, the breakfast favorite of Malaysians, is also eaten at other times. A pancake made from wheat-flour dough, roti canai sometimes incorporates beaten egg and diced onions.

Rojak is a salad of pineapple, cucumber, bean curd, shrimp fritters, and boiled egg, and is served with peanut sauce.

Char kway teow is flat rice noodles stir-fried with minced garlic, fresh prawns, bean sprouts, cockles, and eggs, seasoned with soy sauce and chili paste.

Curry laksa, a noodle dish served in curry, blends boiled chicken, cockles, tofu, and bean sprouts for a surprisingly good treat.

A **steamboat** is the Malaysian version of the hot pot. A steaming cauldron of broth simmers at the table while diners add raw shrimp, chicken, quails' eggs, sea cucumber, and liver to the boiling broth.

AND THE INDONESIAN FAVES

Mie goreng is rice or noodles fried in coconut oil with eggs, meat, tomato, cucumber, shrimp paste, spices, and chilies. This is among the most popular everyday foods in Indonesia. Both nasi goreng and mie goreng are common breakfast dishes.

Nasi campur is a plate of steamed rice with flavorful beef, chicken, mutton, and/or fish, plus a mixture of eggs and/or vegetables, crisp onions, roasted peanuts, and shredded coconut heaped on top.

Rijstaffel (rice table), a sort of Indonesian smorgasbord, is a legacy of the Dutch. In colonial days, a ceremonial rijstaffel could include as many as 35 courses.

> **A KEY CONDIMENT TO INDONESIAN COOKING IS KECAP MANIS, OR SWEET SOY SAUCE.** Pronounced "ketchup," it's the Indonesian origin of the English word.

Today, 10 to 15 courses is the norm. The total meal offers a variety of tastes—some sweet, others spicy, all eaten with steaming hot rice and condiments.

Krupuk is the Indonesian pretzel, a big, crispy, oversize cracker made from fish flakes, crab claws, shrimp paste, or fruit mixed with rice, dough, or sago flour. Krupuk is dried until it looks like thin, hard, colored plastic, then fried in oil. Indonesians use krupuk the way we use bread.

Gado-gado is a healthy warm vegetable salad combining potatoes and other boiled vegetables, a rich peanut sauce, and krupuk.

Sayur nangka is young jackfruit curry made with coconut milk.

DESSERTS

Both Indonesia and Malaysia, being tropical, offer a variety of tropical fruit puddings and frozen desserts. Malaysia's most famous dessert is ABC. ABC stands for air batu campur, which means "ice mix," and consists of a bowl of a delightfully sinful mixture of red bean, cendol (green strands of pandan (screwpine) flavored rice flour), jelly, peanuts, and palm seed kernel topped with a mound of shaved ice, syrup, coconut milk, and corn. Bo bo cha cha is made of sweet potato, yam, and coconut milk.

Cool down and please your sweet tooth in Indonesian establishments with ice-cold es campur (coconut cream, pandan syrup, palm seeds, seaweed jelly, and young coconut, over ice), es teler (sliced jackfruit, avocados, and basil seeds over ice), or pisang goreng es krim (deep-fried bananas with vanilla and chocolate ice cream).

BEVERAGES

A variety of interesting nonalcoholic drinks are enjoyed in these two countries, including many delicious drinks made with coconut. Try es kopyor (iced special coconut) and es kelapa muda (iced young coconut). Both are usually prepared fresh when you order them, with coconut meat and juice, sugar syrup, and a pink cherry-flavored syrup called sirop. Javanese tea, a jasmine tea made with local black tea leaves, is also wonderful, as is es jeruk, a refreshing fruit drink made from fresh-squeezed tangerines and sugar.

Indonesians drink strong Chinese tea with their meals. Powerful coffee (called kopi), introduced by the Dutch in 1699, is grown widely on Java, Bali, and Sumatra, and is served pitch-black, sweet, thick, and rich, with the grounds floating on top. Indonesian kopi is sometimes laced with chicory or chocolate.

As both Malaysia and Indonesia are predominantly Muslim societies, their restaurants don't usually serve alcohol, but generally allow diners to bring in their own. If you can find them, Bintang and Anker are two Indonesian beers (from Dutch recipes). Like the Filipinos, the Javanese make mildly alcoholic tuak (palm toddy), brewed from various palm sugars. There is also Javanese brem, a sweet rice wine, and Balinese arak, a sour-tasting hard liquor usually made from palm tree sap, doctored with sugar or honey to mask its natural flavor.

MALAYSIAN RESTAURANTS

Taste Good

82-18 45th Avenue, Elmhurst
718-898-8001
Subway: G, R, or V to Elmhurst
Ave.
Voted No. 2 in 2002 of the *Village Voice*'s Best & Least Expensive restaurants in New York City. The owners didn't put their resources into the décor.

Penang Malaysian Cuisine

82-24 Broadway, Elmhurst
718-672-7380
Subway: G, R, or V to Elmhurst
Ave.
The Flushing location was Penang's original, where diners lined up for a table. They have since closed the Flushing branch and cloned themselves into a chain, but still serve excellent Malaysian food.

Sentosa

39-07 Prince St., between 39th and Roosevelt avenues in Flushing
718-886-6331
Subway: No. 7 to the Main St.
Sentosa has been around a while, but only recently moved into this attractive new setting.

INDONESIAN RESTAURANTS

Warteg Fortuna

51-24 Roosevelt Ave., Woodside, near corner of 52nd St. & Roosevelt
718-898-2554
Subway: No. 7 to 52nd St. (Lincoln Ave.)
Small and unassuming to the max, with very authentic Indonesian food.

Upi Jaya

76-04 Woodside Ave., Elmhurst
718-458-1807
Subway: No. 7 to 74th St., or E or F to Roosevelt Ave., Jackson Heights
Cute little place with excellent Sumatran fare. The sayur nangka (jackfruit curry) is my favorite.

Beef Redang with Coconut Sambal

INGREDIENTS

1 tablespoon tamarind pulp (available in Indian and Latino markets)

1/4 cup water

3 pounds beef chuck

4 tablespoons oil

2 onions, peeled and diced

6 garlic cloves, peeled and diced

1 tablespoon minced fresh ginger

1 tablespoon finely sliced lemongrass (white part only)

8 dried chilies or 1 tablespoon sambal oelek (hot sauce)

6 whole cardamoms or 1 teaspoon cardamom seeds

1 teaspoon ground cumin

2 teaspoons ground coriander

1/2–1 teaspoon ground galanga (a Southeast Asian member of the ginger family. Sold fresh in ethnic markets)

1/2 teaspoon ground cinnamon

2 cups coconut milk

salt to taste

DIRECTIONS

Mix the tamarind pulp and water together until muddy and smooth. Strain discarding the pulp. Set the water aside. Trim excess fat from the beef and cut the beef into thick strips about the width of your index finger. Heat the oil in a flame-proof casserole and add the onions, garlic, ginger, and lemongrass. Cook over moderate heat until vegetables are fragrant and lightly colored. Add the chilies or sambal oelek, cardamom, cumin, coriander, galanga, and cinnamon. Stir over the heat for 1 minute. Add the beef, coconut milk, and tamarind water. Stir until the mixture comes to a boil, lower the heat, and cook, uncovered, for 2-2 1/2 hours, stirring occasionally. This sauce should be reduced and the oil separated from the sauce. Skim off and discard the oil. Season well with salt. Serve over steamed long-grain rice like jasmine with coconut sambal and green beans.

SERVES 6.

Coconut Sambal

INGREDIENTS

1 cup freshly grated coconut (If you cannot get fresh coconut to grate,
 use 1-1/4 cups shredded coconut, and toss with 2 or 3 tablespoons
 warm water to moisten)

1 teaspoon salt

1 teaspoon sambal oelek or chili paste

2 spring onions, trimmed and finely chopped

a good squeeze of lime or lemon juice

DIRECTIONS

Mix the coconut, salt, chili paste, spring onion, and lemon or lime juice in
a bowl. Serve with redang.

Nasi Goreng

INGREDIENTS

1-1/2 cups cooked, chilled white rice

3 eggs

2 tablespoons vegetable oil

1 onion, chopped

1 leek, chopped

1 garlic clove

2 green chilies, or 1 to 2 teaspoons sambal badjak or sambal oelek

1 teaspoon coriander

1 teaspoon cumin

1/2 pound chicken meat

1/2 pound ground shelled shrimp

3 tablespoons kecap manis (sweet soy sauce)

DIRECTIONS

Cook the rice and set aside. (For best result, cook rice the night before and keep in the fridge overnight.) Beat the eggs and make into a thin omelet. Slice into strips and set aside. Heat the oil in a wok or large frying pan. Add the chopped onion, leek, garlic, and chilies. Fry until the onion is soft. Add the coriander and cumin. Slice chicken into strips and add with the shrimp to the onion mixture. Cook, stirring occasionally, until they are well mixed. Add the rice, kecap manis, and omelet strips and cook for another 5 minutes. Decorate with some of the leftover leek and serve hot.

SERVES 4-6 AS A SIDE DISH.

Central
Asia

⊙ UZBEKISTAN/ TADJIKISTAN
(BUKHARAN JEWISH CUISINE)

BEGINNING WITH THE BREAKUP OF THE
Soviet Union in the early 1990s, thousands of
Bukharan (Central Asian) Jews emigrated to the
United States and Israel. Of those who chose the
U.S., the majority—roughly 40,000—settled in
the Queens neighborhoods of Forest Hills, Kew
Gardens, and Rego Park, sometimes referred to as
"Regoparkistan." They are called Bukharan Jews
because for many centuries Bukhara was the city
where their ancestors lived. Their Judaic
language, called Bukharan, is similar to Farsi.

The ancestors of the Bukharan Jews were Babylonians who migrated eastward after the conquest of Jerusalem by the Romans. Large numbers of Persian Jews migrated to Central Asia in the 1700s, advancing to the Silk Road junction between Persia and China. Since Bukhara, Tashkent, Dushanbe, and Kokand, where the

FRESHLY BAKED LEPESHKA IN BEAUTIFUL BUKHARA IN FOREST HILLS

Bukharan Jews settled, are all along the Silk Road, their food also reflects Turkish, Mongolian, Chinese, Russian, Middle Eastern, Korean, and even Indian influences.

The cuisine emphasizes shish kabobs, soups, cold salads and rice dishes. The dish usually regarded as the Bukharan national dish is called plov or plav or plaf, from the word pilaf. Plov illustrates the Persian influence on this cuisine. It is a basmati rice pilaf with bits of carrot, onion, and other vegetables topped with meat. There are numerous variations of plov, the only immutable ingredient being the rice. There are everyday plovs, holiday plovs, and Sabbath plovs. Carrots are the most standard ingredient—preferably yellow carrots, when obtainable. Meats, vegetables, and eggs are added according to various recipes. Leftover plov from the Sabbath dinner is often eaten for breakfast with eggs.

The traditional meal served in a Bukharan home consists of salad, shish kabob, and plov, all served separately. Desserts are traditionally fruits like grapes and melons, and halvah, a sweet made from ground sesame seeds and honey or sugar.

Both types of bread favored by

Bukharans are known as tandosri, referring to the type of oven in which they are baked. At Beautiful Bukhara in Forest Hills, the oven resembles a closet that has been tiled both on the interior and exterior. The baker actually walks in to arrange his loaves on the shelves. Lepeshka, the national bread of Bukhara, is a puffy, Frisbee-sized loaf with a pattern stamped in the middle, studded with black and white sesame seeds and/or onions. The alternative is non tiki, a bowl-shaped matzoh like bread. Non tiki is denser and harder than matzoh, and is studded with spices like cumin and coriander. Not much of a taste sensation in and of itself, but a nice crunchy foil with the savories.

Every culture we've encountered seems to have its beloved versions of dumplings and turnovers, and Bukharans are no exception. For lunch or a light supper you can't beat 'em. There are three main varieties in the Bukharan repertoire. The fillings are all rather similar—lots of onions with ground beef, chicken, or fish. Cheburekes, the Crimean version, are deep fried. Uzbek mantu is boiled. Samsa (not unlike Indian samosas) are a little spicier than the others and baked in a flaky (if greasy) pastry casing. All three are tasty, and definitely enhanced by tkemali sauce, a slightly spicy sauce based on pickled prunes, which serves as Bukharan ketchup.

Central Asians eat a lot of salads. We have been told that in recent times there's been a lot of trade and travel between Korea and Uzbekistan, and that when Uzbekis go out to eat, Korean food is the cuisine of choice. Many Korean dishes have infiltrated Uzbeki menus, especially Korean carrot salad, sometimes called morkovcha. This is a tangy and refreshing finely shredded carrot salad heavily laden with garlic and other less easily identified flavors. Baba ganoush, popular throughout the Mediterranean, is another mainstay; the Bukharans like theirs creamy and smoky. "Uzbeki" salad is made of chopped tomatoes and cucumbers with onions and dill (similar to Turkish coban). Bukharans also eat several types of cubed beetroot salads. I haven't encountered these on restaurant menus, but they are readily found in delis catering to Bukharans and Russians.

Soup is an essential part of the meal. Lagman is a tomatoey beef and noodle soup flavored with pepper and dill. Shurpa is another hearty, meaty soup, usually made from lamb (sometimes beef) with a mélange of vegetables. Pelmeni is dumpling soup. The tortellini-like dumplings can be filled with beef, chicken, or fish. Harcho is rice soup with meat. Hasib, a Bukharan sausage made of a mixture of meats and rice, achieves its characteristically smooth texture through the addition of beef spleen.

Kebabs, ubiquitous throughout Eastern Europe and Central Asia, are a mainstay of the Bukharan diet as well. They are seasoned with salt, garlic, cumin, coriander, and sometimes cinnamon. You can find kebabs made with several cuts of lamb, lula (ground meat), beef, chicken, veal, fish, vegetables, a variety of organ meats, and, occasionally, lamb testicles. One restaurant in Rego Park, Cheburechnaya, serves lamb fat kebabs. Another alternates small pieces of fat between chunks of liver in its veal liver kebabs. Bukharans must not have the same fear of fat as the average American.

Kebabs are eaten with vegetables, onion topping, and French fries. Garlic fries, a delicious variant on plain fries, are usually available. Ask for tkemali sauce for a little added zip, and if bread isn't

> ### NEVER ON SATURDAY
>
> Most Bukharan restaurants observe the Sabbath by closing early on Fridays and reopening, if at all, after sundown on Saturdays.

brought automatically, order some.

BEVERAGES

Tea is the traditional beverage of choice, either green, black, or black tea with lemon and sugar. Although we noticed many of our fellow diners drinking Snapple tea, there are several soft drinks popular with Central Asians, including tarhun, a carbonated drink with digestive properties based on tarragon extract; dushes, a pear-flavored soft drink; and borzhomi, a Russian brand of mineral water widely available where Bukharans eat.

DESSERTS

I've never been wowed by the desserts served at the Regoparkistan restaurants. Maybe it's me. I find them dense, heavy, and uninteresting. Halvah, the sesame honey candy, is popular, as is lavz, a confection made from sugar and crushed nuts. They also eat

INSTRUMENT USED IN LEPESHKA PREPERATION FOR MAKING
DECORATIVE IMPRESSIONS IN CENTER OF LOAF

baklava, the universal Mediterranean treat. I've never been served an outstanding baklava in a Bukharan establishment, probably because, in observing the kosher dietary laws, a restaurant serving meat doesn't use butter. Bukharans also eat a sweet samsa, similar to the savory samsa but filled with nuts and honey. And they have an uncommon fondness for marshmallow fluff. They spread it on lepeshka and eat it as a sweet snack or dessert.

The food stores that serve the Bukharan community are of special interest, not only for the ingredients they offer but as a source of first-rate take-out foods. They bill themselves as "European delis" rather than Central Asian or Bukharan, and carry products from Russia, Eastern Europe, and Central Asia as well as locally prepared delicacies. (Most of them bill themselves as "the best European delicatessen." "Prove it," I say.) Some of these stores are kosher, some not. They all sell lepeshka and other interesting breads, smoked fish, cured meats, ethnic dairy products, and imported candies and cookies.

Monya & Misha Delicatessen on

108th St. in Forest Hills offers a wonderful selection of unusual freshly prepared salads like whitefish with beets, assorted meat dishes, heavenly homemade blintzes, and blintz wrappers ready to fill. Their take-out foods are at a counter on the left as you walk in. A & R International Food Delicatessen has an excellent selection of breads, and, if you arrive at the right time, killer sirniki (fried cheese balls) as well as a variety of salads and pickled vegetables. A & D European Delicatessen in Rego Park also features homemade foods like mantu (Uzbek dumplings) and a range of pickled items, like pickled apples. All of these stores have great possibilities for take-out meals, although some gesturing and pointing (and maybe tasting) may be involved. Be prepared to fight tooth and nail for attention if these stores are busy. There is no such thing as a polite "No, after you" in these establishments.

BUKHARAN RESTAURANTS

(All of the following are kosher)

Salute Restaurant
63-42 108th St., Forest Hills
718-275-6860
Subway: E or F to Forest Hills/Continental Ave., Q2 3 north to 63rd Dr. & 108th St.
Small sit-down restaurant decorated like a micro-mini catering hall. Stick-to-your-ribs food.

Beautiful Bukhara
64-47 108 St., Forest Hills
718-275-2220
Subway: E or F to Forest Hills/Continental Ave., Q 23 north to 64th Rd. & 108th St.
My favorite for samsas. Stop by for lepeshka and non tiki straight from the tandoor.

Cheburechnaya
92-09 63rd Dr., Rego Park
718-897-9080
Subway: G or V to 63rd Dr., walk south on 63rd Dr.
Great kebabs (including lamb testicles, if you dare) in no-frills surroundings.

Arzu Restaurant
101-05 Queens Blvd. (between 102nd St & 67th Rd.), Rego Park
718-830-3335
Subway: G or V to 67th Ave.
Another excellent choice for food, devoid of atmosphere.

Registan
65-37 99th St., Rego Park
718-459-1638
Subway: G or V to 63rd Dr. Exit
subway on north side of Queens
Blvd. Walk north on 65th Rd. to
99th St.
Tiny and authentic.

Crystal International Foods, Inc.
94-09 63rd Dr., Rego Park
718-830-0163
Subway: G or V to 63rd Dr., walk
south on 63rd Dr.

EUROPEAN DELIS
CATERING TO CENTRAL
ASIANS AND RUSSIANS

*M & M and Son, Inc. (Monya
& Misha)*
64-46 108th St., Forest Hills
718-459-0180
Subway: E or F to Forest
Hills/Continental Ave., Q 23 north
to 64th Rd. & 108th St.

*A & R International Food
Delicatessen*
63-46 108th St., Forest Hills
718-459-3956
Subway: E or F to Forest
Hills/Continental Ave., Q 23 north
to 63rd Rd. & 108th St.

*A & D Best International
Delicatessen*
93-07 63rd Dr., Rego Park
718-997-0501
Subway: G or V to 63rd Dr., walk
south on 63rd Dr.

Shurpa *(Hearty spiced lamb soup from Central Asia)*

This rich, aromatic soup is beautiful, with its colorful root vegetables; it's superb as a winter meal.

═══

INGREDIENTS

1/4 cup olive oil

1-1/2 pounds stewing lamb, cut into 1-inch chunks

1 cup onions, chopped

10 cups beef stock

1 large turnip, peeled and cut into a 1/2-inch dice

1 large zucchini, cut into a 1/2-inch dice

2 carrots, cut into a 1/2-inch dice

2 big green bell peppers, cored, seeded, and cut into strips

1-1/2 pounds tomatoes, peeled, seeded, and chopped

1-1/2 teaspoons cumin

1/2 teaspoon hot pepper flakes

1 teaspoon ground coriander

1 16-ounce can chick-peas, drained

salt, to taste

3 tablespoons white vinegar

garnish: 1/2 cup chopped fresh cilantro

DIRECTIONS

In a large Dutch oven, brown the meat in the hot oil over high heat for about 5 minutes, stirring occasionally. Stir in the onions and cook 5 or so more minutes, until the onions are softened and have taken on color. Spoon off all the fat that you can, pour in the stock, and bring to a boil. Reduce the heat, cover, and simmer for about 1-1/2 hours. Refrigerate the soup, preferably overnight, so you can easily remove the fat. About an hour before serving, start chopping vegetables. Bring the skimmed soup to a boil over medium heat, then add the turnip, zucchini, carrots, peppers, tomatoes, cumin, hot pepper flakes, coriander, and chick-peas. Cook, covered, for 30 minutes. Salt to taste, then stir in the vinegar. Cover and let stand for 15 minutes. Ladle into bowls and garnish with lots of finely minced cilantro. If you make this soup ahead and chill it, you can scrape off the excess fat from the top before serving.

SERVES 8.

Bukharan Salad

INGREDIENTS

6 scallions

6 cucumbers

6 ripe medium tomatoes

3 sprigs of coriander

juice of 1 large lemon

3 tablespoons good quality olive oil

salt and pepper to taste

DIRECTIONS

Trim the scallions, discarding the green stems. Peel and halve the cucumbers and scoop out their seeds. Chop the cucumbers, tomatoes, and scallions to a 1/4-inch dice. Wash and dry the coriander. Finely mince it and stir it into the vegetables. Add the lemon juice, oil, and salt and pepper. Stir well and chill. Serve in small bowls.

SERVES 4-6.

Uzbek Plov

INGREDIENTS

2 pounds boneless shoulder or leg of lamb, with some fat (the fat lends
    flavor to the dish)
2 tablespoons olive oil
2 large onions, julienned
3 large carrots, julienned
2-1/2 cups raw rice
4-1/2 cups boiling water
1 teaspoon avjar (Turkish red pepper and garlic puree, available in
    Russian and Turkish food stores)
3 teaspoons salt
1/8 teaspoon saffron, steeped in 2 tablespoons boiling water for 10 minutes
freshly ground black pepper, to taste
raw onion, sliced paper-thin

DIRECTIONS

Cut the lamb into chunks. Heat the oil over high heat in a large Dutch
oven, then stir in the lamb and brown on all sides. Remove to a plate and
keep warm in a 200-degree oven. Stir onions and carrots into the
remaining fat, adding a little more olive oil if necessary. Cook over
medium heat for 10-15 minutes, until tender but not browned. Return the
lamb to the pot and add the raw rice. Cook, stirring, for 5 minutes, or until
the rice begins to turn golden brown. Pour in the boiling water, stirring to
mix well. Add the avjar, salt, saffron tea, and black pepper. Cover and cook
over low heat for 20 minutes, or until rice is done. Garnish liberally with
raw onion.

SERVES 6-8.

◉ AFGHANISTAN

It was a toss-up, deciding whether to place Afghanistan in Central Asia or South Asia, culinarily speaking.

Both geographically and gastronomically, it's a tough call. Queens's Afghan population numbered 4,364 in 2000, and is mostly centered in Flushing. Their cuisine reflects influences from neighbors in the Middle East, Central Asia, India, and the Far East. And there is internal diversity as well, with tribes like the Pashtuns, Tajiks, and Uzbeks having their own specialties.

The mainstays of the Afghan diet are their version of naan (tandoori bread), basmati rice pilaf, and kebabs. Sound familiar? What gives their food its identifiable Afghan flavor is a seasoning blend called char masala, made from cinnamon, cloves, cumin, and black cardamom, used especially in rice pilafs. Lamb kebabs sprinkled generously with fiery ground red pepper are a specialty of the city of Jalalabad.

In Afghan eateries, as in Bukharan ones, you might find mantu, those savory meat-filled pasta purses, as well as several fried pastries akin to Indian samosas and pakoras. Afghan meatball soup gets its distinctive taste from dill weed, while a mushroom stew might be seasoned with turmeric, fennel seeds, and ground ginger. Sweet and spicy combinations, such as coriander seeds and chilies, are sometimes added to stews or meatballs. Pickled condiments and chutneys are an essential part of every meal. The favored drinks are ginger tea and doogh, a minted cucumber and yogurt drink.

AFGHAN RESTAURANTS

Kabul Kebab House
42-51 Main St. (between Cherry &
Franklin), Flushing
718-461-1919
Subway: No. 7 to Main St., Q 44
east to Elder Ave. if you don't want
to walk

Choopan Kebab House
43-27 Main St., Flushing
718-539-3180
Subway: No. 7 to Main St., Q 44
east to Elder Ave. if you don't want
to walk

Afghan Kebab House IV
74-16 37 Ave. (between 73d and
74th Sts.), Jackson Heights
718-565-0471
Subway: No. 7 to 74th St. or E or
F to Roosevelt Ave. / Jackson
Heights

Bahar
82-19 Queens Blvd., Elmhurst
718-426-5822
Subway: G or V to Grand Ave.

Balkh Shish Kabab House
23-10 31st St., Astoria
718-721-5020
Subway: N to Astoria Blvd.

⊙ TIBET

SOMEWHERE IN THE CENSUS'S 269,855 "unclassified or not reported" are a bunch of Tibetans. I found approximately 100 listings each in the Queens phone book under the names Sherpa and Lama, the Smiths and Joneses of Tibet. I'm sure that's only the tip of the iceberg.

There is only one Tibetan restaurant in Queens, with little signs of this cuisine catching on, so I won't dwell on it. Momos, steamed Tibetan dumplings, are this culture's culinary high point. They are filled with meat and/or vegetables and accompanied by a dipping sauce. Most of the other Tibetan fare that has been exported stands somewhere between a mild curry and a slightly spicy stir-fry.

A Tibetan specialty I've read about and don't care to try is yak blood cubes, which are made by drawing 0.25 kilograms of blood from the veins of a yak. The blood is then poured into a pan and boiled on a slow fire until it solidifies, and then cut into cubes. Hot butter is poured on them and white sugar is added. As far as I can tell, yak blood cubes haven't made it to Queens.

Po cha, Tibetan butter tea, is the most typical Tibetan drink. It's a bit of an acquired taste, but not bad once you get used to it.

TIBETAN RESTAURANT

Tibetan Yak
72-20 Roosevelt Ave. (between 72
& 73 Sts.), Jackson Heights
718 779-1119
Subway: E or F to Roosevelt Ave.,
Jackson Heights, or No. 7 to 74th
St.
Being the only one of its kind in
Queens makes it worth a try.

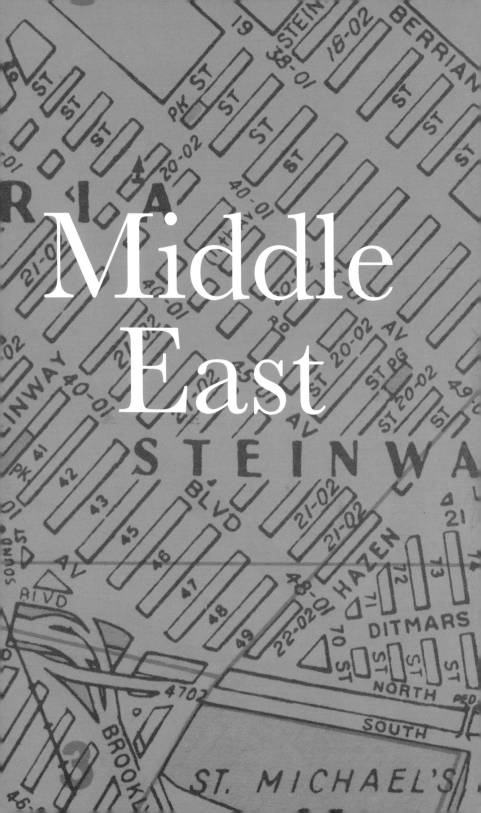

Middle
East

"The souk" might now be an apt moniker for Steinway Street in Astoria, which was once nicknamed "the World's Longest Department Store." The stretch between 30th Street and Astoria Boulevard has been reinvigorated by businesses catering to a Middle Eastern clientele. It is dotted with cafes serving coffee, tea, and shisha, the apple-flavored tobacco smoked in a hookah pipe, as well as Middle Eastern merchants, eateries, food stores, a mosque, and an Arab cultural center. Although many of the restaurants and cafés describe themselves as offering Middle Eastern cuisine, in reality they are mainly owned and operated by Egyptians.

⊙ EAT LIKE AN EGYPTIAN

EGYPTIAN IS ONE CUISINE THAT, HAPPILY, is as healthy as it is delicious—think Mediterranean Diet.

Its flavors depend heavily on ingredients like herbs, garlic, lemon, and vegetables. The preferred fats are olive oil or, as in South Asia, ghee (clarified butter), samneh in Arabic. Baharat, which includes cinnamon, cumin, allspice, and paprika, is the characteristic flavoring used to season meats.

As in so many cultures, the "staff of life," called aysh in Arabic, is eaten with everything. The most common is a type of pita made either with refined white flour, known as aysh shami, or with coarse whole wheat, aysh baladi. Stuffed with any of several fillings, it becomes the Egyptian sandwich. Aysh shams is bread made from leavened dough allowed to rise in the sun, while plain aysh comes in long, skinny, French-style loaves.

Another major component of the Egyptian diet is fava beans, or foul (pronounced fool) medames, known for their nutritional value.

They can be cooked several ways: in foul medames, the whole beans are boiled, with vegetables if desired, and then mashed with onions, tomatoes, and spices. This mixture is often served with an egg for breakfast, and without the egg for other meals. A similar sauce, cooked down into a paste and stuffed into aysh baladi, serves as the filling for sandwiches. Alternatively, foul beans are soaked, minced, mixed with spices, formed into patties (called ta'miyya in Cairo, falaafil in Alexandria, and falafel in Tel Aviv), and deep-fried. These patties, garnished with tomatoes, lettuce, and tahini sauce, are stuffed into aysh.

MEZZE

Mezze, a kind of appetizers, are one of the most appealing parts of Egyptian cuisine. In fact, ready-made tahini, hummus, and baba ganoush are such common commodities on supermarket shelves that they hardly seem like foreign food. Tahini is made from sesame-seed paste. Tahini mixed with oil and seasoned with garlic or chili and lemon can be served alone, but when combined with mashed eggplant and served as a dip or sauce for salads, it's called baba ganoush. Chick-peas are added to the tahini to make hummus bi tahini. Tahini also forms the base for many general purpose sauces served with fish and meats, and replaces mayonnaise on Egyptian sandwiches. Turshi includes a variety of vegetables soaked in spicy brine.

SOUPS AND SALADS

Molokhiyya is a distinctively Egyptian leafy green summer vegetable, from which a thick soup is made by stewing the chopped leaves in chicken stock, with or without meat. It is sometimes served with crushed bread over rice. In addition to molokhiyya, the Egyptians make a variety of soups (shurbah) from meat (lahhma), vegetables (khudaar), and fish (samak). It is perfectly acceptable to dip your aysh in them.

Salads (salata) can be made of greens, tomatoes, potatoes, or eggs, as well as with beans and yogurt.

MAIN COURSES

In Egypt, as in most of the world, meat is a luxury used in small amounts, cooked with vegetables, and served with or over rice. But restaurants serve mostly meat dishes.

Torly, a mixed vegetable casserole or stew, is usually made with lamb, or occasionally with beef, onions, potatoes, beans, and peas. Long-simmering stews or sauces called tagines are a universal North African and Middle Eastern dish. Tagine refers to the finished simmered dish (meat, chicken, fish, fresh vegetables, or fruits) seasoned with spices and slowly stewed in a covered earthenware dish. Tagine also refers to the earthenware pot, topped with a conical lid, in which this dish is made. The cooking liquid is a combination of water and olive oil or seasoned smen (clarified butter), or broth. The finished product is soft and tender and traditionally eaten with the hands. Popular tagines include chicken with preserved lemons, ginger, and saffron; fresh fish with tomato sauce and cumin; and lamb with prunes, cinnamon, and rose water.

To make Egyptian-style kebab, cooks season chunks of lamb in onion, marjoram, and lemon juice, and then roast them on a spit over an open fire. Kufta is ground lamb flavored with spices and onions that's rolled into long narrow "meatballs" and roasted like kebab, with which it's often served.

Egyptians serve freshwater fish, seagoing fish, and shellfish under the general term samak.

Ruzz, or rice, is a Middle Eastern staple that's often cooked with nuts, onions, vegetables, or small amounts of meat. Bataatis (potatoes) are usually fried but can also be found boiled or stuffed. Egyptians stuff green vegetables with various rice mixtures; wara' enab, for example, is made from boiled grape leaves filled with small amounts of spiced rice with or without ground meat. Westerners often know them by the Greek name of dolmadas or dolmas.

Native cheese (gibna) comes in two varieties: gibna beida, similar to feta, and gibna rumy, a sharp, hard, pale yellow cheese. These are the cheeses typically used in salads and sandwiches.

AND FOR DESSERT . . .

Not all Middle Eastern restaurants in Queens offer dessert. Egyptians are more likely to finish a meal with fresh or dried fruits, especially dates, unless it's a special occasion. Some restaurants get desserts from a fabulous Palestinian-owned bakery called Laziza on the Little Egypt stretch of Steinway Street. As in the rest of the Mediterranean, desserts of pastry or puddings are usually drenched in honey syrup. Baklava (phyllo dough, honey, and nuts) is one of the less sweet; fatir are pancakes stuffed with everything from eggs to apricots; and basbousa, quite sweet, is made of semolina pastry soaked in honey and topped with hazelnuts. Umm ali is raisin cake soaked in milk and served hot. Kanafa is a dish of batter "strings" fried on a hot grill and stuffed with nuts, meats, or sweets. Egyptian rice pudding is called mahallabiyya and is served topped with pistachios.

BEVERAGES
COFFEE

The most exotic arrivals of the Middle Eastern culture on Steinway Street are the coffee cafes that double as hookah bars. Developed and popularized in the Middle East, the drinking of ahwa (coffee) remains a strong tradition, and local coffee houses cater to men who come to drink coffee, discuss politics, play tawla (backgammon), listen to "Oriental" (Egyptian) music, and smoke the hookah.

Turkish coffee is made from finely powdered beans brewed in a small pot. As the water begins to boil, the grounds float to the surface in a dark foam; the ahwa is

> SHISHA, TOBACCO MIXED WITH FRUIT, MOLASSES, AND HONEY, IS USED WHEN SMOKING OUT OF A WATER PIPE CALLED A HOOKAH OR NARGILLE (PRONOUNCED NAR-GEELY).
>
> The tobacco is a ground-up mixture of dried fruit pulp, flavored molasses, and fresh tobacco leaves. The list of flavors reads something like an ice cream parlor menu, including apple, apricot, strawberry, cappuccino, mint, cherry, and grape, and it just goes on and on. Smoking hookahs (or anything else) indoors in a public place is strictly forbidden under New York City law; however, the New York City Department of Health, the agency responsible for enforcing the ban, seems to turn a blind eye to this cultural phenomenon.

brought to you still in the pot and poured into a demitasse. The heavier grounds sink to the bottom of the cup, and the lighter ones form a foam on the top, the mark of a perfectly brewed cup. Sip carefully to avoid the grounds in the bottom of the cup. (If you don't like the foam, you can blow it aside under the guise of cooling your drink.)

Although Turkish coffee has a reputation for being tart, its actual flavor depends on the mix of beans used in the grind; the larger the percentage of Arabica, the sweeter and more chocolate the flavor. Ahwa comes in several versions: ahwa sada is black, ahwa ariha is lightly sweetened with sugar, ahwa

mazboot is moderately sweetened, and ahwa ziyada is very sweet. You must specify the amount of sugar at the time you order, for it's sweetened in the pot. Ahwa is never served with cream.

TEA AND OTHER HOT DRINKS

Shay bil na'na', or mint tea, is a refreshing change from after-dinner coffee. Dried mint is mixed with tea leaves, and the mixture is brewed like regular tea and served in a glass. Kakoow bil laban (hot chocolate) is drunk during the winter, as is sahlab, a thick liquid that tastes like a cross between Ovaltine and oatmeal. Karkaday, a clear, bright red drink, is made by steeping dried hibiscus flowers, sweetened to taste, and served either hot or cold. Egyptians claim this drink calms the nerves.

EGYPTIAN/MIDDLE EASTERN RESTAURANTS

Most serve no alcohol, but some will allow you to bring your own.

Mombar

25-22 Steinway St. (between 25th & 28th avenues), Astoria
718-726-2356
Subway: N, W to 30th Ave.
Owner Moustafa Rahman lovingly turned his restaurant into a work of Egyptian outsider art. It's a feast for the eyes as well as the tummy. There are no menus, and the southern Egyptian offerings change according to whim. When Moustafa is in the right mood, a meal here is sublime. Pricey for an ethnic restaurant, but when Moustafa is in top form, worth every penny.

Kebab Café

25-12 Steinway St., Astoria
718-728-9858
Subway: N, W to Astoria Blvd.
This small restaurant, run by Ali

Rahman, Moustafa's brother, lacks the visual charm of Mombar, but gets high marks for hospitality and offers up some pretty fine eating. As at Mombar, there are no menus; expect to be pleasantly surprised by what Ali whips up—but not so pleasantly by your check, which may be steep for the modest surroundings.

Sabry's

24-25 Steinway St., Astoria
718-721-9010
Subway: N, W to Astoria Blvd.
Egyptian-style seafood and Middle Eastern sides. Very fresh fish. Try the tagine.

Eastern Nights

25-35 Steinway St., Astoria
718-204-7608
Subway: N, W to Astoria Blvd.

Quick and Easy Foul

INGREDIENTS
1 can of fava (foul) beans
olive oil
lemon juice
salt, pepper to taste

DIRECTIONS
Heat the beans in a saucepan, mashing them against the side of the pan. When they're hot and thoroughly mashed, add lemon juice, olive oil, and seasoning to taste. Eat immediately with bread.

Turli *(Egyptian casserole of mixed vegetables)*

INGREDIENTS

1/2 pound okra

3 tablespoons vegetable oil

1 pound beef, cut into bite-size cubes

1 medium eggplant, peeled and cubed

1/2 pound string beans, halved lengthwise

1 cup frozen peas, thawed

2-3 potatoes, peeled and diced

5-7 pearl onions, peeled

1 teaspoon dried mint

1 hot pepper, chopped very fine

salt and pepper

DIRECTIONS

Wash and dry the okra well. Peel ridges very thinly, then peel the cap by turning okra around a knife, removing the hard edges. The top of the okra should look conical.

Heat 1 tablespoon oil in large skillet. Fry meat in hot oil until the juice is reabsorbed. Remove meat from pan and place in Dutch oven or large saucepan. Add eggplant, string beans, peas, potatoes, and onions to the skillet with remaining 2 tablespoons oil. Sauté. Add vegetables to meat, together with mint, hot pepper, and seasoning. Cover with water and cook over very low flame until meat and vegetables are tender (about 1-1/2 to 2 hours).

⊙ISRAEL

ISRAEL IS ANOTHER MIDDLE EASTERN country with a large community in Queens, mainly around Kew Gardens Hills. Some would argue that Israel doesn't have a cuisine, just a mishmash of culinary influences from the various parts of the world from which the Jewish settlers emigrated. That may be true, but as long as there are Queens restaurants that serve food identified as Israeli, in my book, they have a cuisine. Derivative or not (to paraphrase a certain jazz great) if it tastes good it is good.

The strongest influence on Israeli cuisine is pan-Middle Eastern food. Like Indians and Pakistanis, New York's Arabs and Israelis comfortably patronize many of the same stores without incident, although they mostly open shops in different neighborhoods. Little Israel occupies (you should pardon the expression) eastern Main Street from approximately 68th Drive to Union Turnpike, in a neighborhood known as Kew Gardens Hills. This is also home to a large non-Israeli Orthodox Jewish community.

Foods common to the Middle East—olives and olive oil, wheat,

PAULA STEVENS DISPLAYING HER BUREKAS

chick-peas, yogurt—play a central role in Israeli cuisine. Couscous, the beads of pasta used as a staple and in salad, and matbucha, a salad of cooked red pepper and tomatoes, trace their provenance to the Maghreb (Morocco, Algeria, and Tunisia) nations of North Africa. The origins of falafel are Egyptian. Sharwarma (the Israeli version of the gyro or döner kebab) first came from Turkey, as did the famous "Israeli salad" of cucumbers and tomatoes in distinctively small pieces.

Jewish dietary laws also exert a strong influence, including the separation of milk and meat and the aversion to foods like pork and shellfish. The prohibition against pork is another commonality Israelis share with their Muslim neighbors.

Israelis have a special way with spices like cumin, za'atar, and sumac. Za'atar is a Middle Eastern spice blend with a flavor similar to Syrian hyssop (likely the hyssop referenced in the Bible), which grows wild in the region. It's made by mixing sumac, thyme leaves, white sesame seeds, and salt, and can be used as a tabletop condiment. Sumac is a very popular condiment in Turkey and Iran, where the ground fruits are

> **FOR A NICE APPETIZER,** cut pita bread into wedges, sprinkle with za'atar and olive oil, and bake for 5 minutes at 350°. This is also good sprinkled on thinly sliced onions with a bit of vegetable oil and used on sandwiches and salads.

liberally sprinkled over rice. Mixed with freshly cut onions, sumac is frequently eaten as an appetizer. The well-known Turkish fast food specialty döner kebab is sometimes flavored with sumac powder.

There's no better place to explore Israeli spices than at Pereg on Main Street. It offers a wide range of loose, high-quality herbs and spices, particularly those favored in Middle Eastern cooking. It also sells many of its own spice blends labeled for specific dishes or styles of cooking, and stocks its own line of premixed spice blends (often with nuts) for use in creating spreads or no-brainer rice and pasta dishes. Just cook up some rice or pasta, stir in some of Pereg's blends, and you have an instant exotic dish. The store is very liberal in allowing you to sample its wares

(consider a visit equivalent to a light snack). For a little extra insurance, it offers a comprehensive range of products for warding off the "evil eye."

Israeli restaurants in Queens mostly have the look and feel of falafel equivalents to pizzerias, with a few exceptions. They feature the Israeli adaptations of various Middle Eastern foods like kebabs, falafel, salads, dips, and burekas, the Middle Eastern answer to the empanada. Many also serve kosher pizza, but it's best to focus on the more Mediterranean fare. The only reason I can think of to eat kosher pizza is if you are kosher. (What makes pizza kosher is the use of kosher cheese. What makes cheese kosher is the absence of rennet, an animal enzyme used in non-kosher cheeses.) If a restaurant bills itself as "glatt" kosher, it means that it serves meat. If the sign says "dairy," or kosher without the word "glatt," it's vegetarian. Kosher restaurants serving meat don't serve dairy, and vice versa. Vegetables and fish are considered pareve, meaning they can swing either way.

RESTAURANTS AND PURVEYORS

All of the following close early on Fridays and remain closed until after sundown on Saturdays, in observance of the Jewish Sabbath.

Pereg Gourmet
66-69 Main St., Flushing
718-261-6767
Subway: E, F to 71st Ave.-
Continental; Q 65A bus to Main St.
Fantastic resource for Israeli and Middle Eastern spices.

Paula Stevens Ltd.
63-79 Saunders St., Rego Park
718-459-7276
Subway: V, G to 63rd Dr.; walk one block south on 63rd to Saunders St., and turn left onto Saunders. Call it burekas-r-us—this one-woman operation makes all manner of burekas by hand, including (but not limited to) potato, cheese, spinach, and mushroom. The owner is a Sephardic Jew from Argentina.

Grill Point
69-54 Main St., Flushing
718-261-7077
Subway: E, F to 71st Ave.-
Continental; then Q 65A bus to Main St.
Casual spot for Israeli and Middle Eastern cuisine.

Shimon's
71-24 Main St., Flushing
718-793-1491
Subway: E, F to 71st Ave.-
Continental; then Q 65A bus to Main St.
Kosher pizza, falafel, and meatless Israeli specialties.

Naomi's Kosher Pizza
68-28 Main St.
718-520-8754
Subway: E, F to 71st Ave.-
Continental; then Q 65A bus to Main St.
Falafel, burekas, and Mediterranean delicacies.

Colbeh Restaurant
68-34 Main St., Flushing
718-268-8181
Subway: E, F to 71st Ave.-
Continental; then Q 63A bus to Main St.
The most upscale restaurant on this list, with branches in Manhattan and Great Neck, Colbeh caters to an Israeli clientele with offerings that reflect Persia as much as the Middle East.

Matbucha *(Cooked red pepper and tomato salad)*

INGREDIENTS

2 pounds red peppers
4 pounds soft cooking tomatoes
1/2 cup oil
1 tablespoon sweet paprika
1/2 teaspoon salt
3 small dried chili peppers (or cayenne pepper)
3 teaspoons crushed garlic

DIRECTIONS

Place red peppers on an open flame. Turn the peppers until they are blackened on all sides. Place peppers in a plastic bag and let cool.

Place tomatoes in a deep bowl and poor boiling water over them. After a few minutes, remove from water and peel. Cut tomatoes in half and squeeze out the juice. Chop into large pieces. Put oil and chopped tomatoes into a large pot.

Place blackened peppers under running water and peel them. Cut the peppers into thin strips. Add peppers to the pot with the tomatoes. Add the spices and chopped garlic. Cook on high heat until the mixture begins to stick to the pot. Reduce the heat and cook for about half an hour, until hardly any liquid is left in the pot. Place in a storage container and let cool.

⊙ TURKEY

QUEENS'S TURKISH POPULATION IS centered around Sunnyside in western Queens. It's a relatively small community, with only a little over 3,000 on the 2000 census, but its contribution to Queens deliciousness is significant.

For all cuisines, geography is destiny. Culinary influences pass freely between geographic neighbors without need of passport. That said, some countries are influenced and others do more of the influencing. When it comes to the gastronomic balance of trade, Turkey has a big surplus. Turkish cuisine is at the crossroad of the Far East and the Mediterranean, which mirrors a long and complex history of Turkish migration from the steppes of central Asia (where they mingled with the Chinese) to Europe (where they exerted influence all the way to Vienna). The word yogurt is a Turkish word. The Yiddish word pastrami derives from the Turkish pastirma, meaning dried spiced beef. Throughout the Middle East, everyone drinks Turkish coffee, even if they don't call it that.

Turkish cuisine relies on recipes that are centuries old. Ancient Greeks introduced wine cultivation in Anatolia, eastern Turkey. The Persians introduced sweets, sugar, and rice. Skewered and roasted meats, the famous shish kebab, show the nomadic heritage, as do flatbreads that are baked on an overturned griddle called a sac, similar to a flattened wok. Yogurt, a Turkish invention, made its way north to Bulgaria and Eastern Europe during the Ottoman occupation. Olive oil production is thousands of years old and part of the whole Mediterranean culture.

The most common seasonings

SPICES OF THE MIDDLE EAST

are dill, mint, parsley, cinnamon, garlic, and the lemony sumac. Yogurt is a common side condiment. Another southern condiment is Aleppo pepper flakes, or pul biber. This semi-moist, hot, flaked red pepper is sprinkled on foods before eating. Ajvar is a puree of sweet red peppers available canned or in jars in Turkish delis, and can be used as a dip, condiment, or in all sorts of ways by the creative cook.

Turkish cooks have at least 40 ways to prepare eggplant. Strings of dried, hollowed-out eggplant, one of the most unique, and reconstituted and stuffed with rice in winter.

BREAKFAST

Turks will typically eat fresh tomatoes, white cheese, black olives, bread with honey and preserves, and sometimes an egg for breakfast. Ekmek is a puffy round Turkish bread. Simit are sesame bread rings. Hemsin, listed below, is a Turkish bakery and restaurant that serves a traditional breakfast as well as lunch and dinner. Try its breakfast plate for the Turkish works.

LUNCH

You'll also find pideler (Turkish pizza) at Hemsin. This is street food in Turkey, but here it's the perfect lunch: a thin, crusty, pitalike bread stuffed with various combinations of Turkish meats, sausages, veggies, and cheeses. Kebab sandwiches are another popular alternative.

WHAT'S FOR DINNER?

Turks, like other Middle Easterners, begin their dinners with appetizers. Here they're called souguk (cold) or sicak (hot) mezeler (appetizers). They make their own versions of the universal ones like hummus, baba ganoush, and stuffed grape leaves, but also serve some that are unique to Turkey. Look for acli ezme (spicy mashed peppers with tomatoes, onions, parsley, walnuts, and spices), eggplant in olive oil (stuffed baby eggplant), borek (very thin phyllo dough stuffed with cheese, meat, or vegetables), stuffed cheese sticks (sigari), and coban (shepherd's salad), to name but a few. Cured meats like pastirma (air-dried spiced beef) and sucuk (beef sausage) are popular. With any luck there will be a combination plate that allows you to sample several, always accompanied by the wonderful bread.

MAIN DISHES

Kebabs are a mainstay of the Turkish diet, and a nod to the Turks' nomadic heritage. The popular döner kebab, the Turkish version of the gyro, is made by stacking thin marinated slices of lamb (sometimes alternating with beef) on a vertical skewer for grilling. Isender kebabs are a kind of döner kebab prepared from thinly cut grilled lamb basted with tomato sauce over diced pieces of pita bread and generously slathered with melted butter and yogurt. Hunkar begendi (sultan's delight) is a classic Turkish dish made with baked chunks of meat (usually lamb) served on a creamy bed of eggplant puree that includes kasseri cheese and more closely resembles a rich white sauce than a vegetable.

BEVERAGES

Ayran, or Turkish buttermilk, is a white, creamy, refreshing mixture of water, yogurt, and salt, sometimes with the addition of mint or other herbs. It's considered a summer drink in Turkey, although some drink it in winter. Ayran is called tahn in Armenia, doogh in Afghanistan and Iran, and lassi in India.

Boza is a creamy Turkish drink made with powdered chick-peas, cinnamon, and sugar. This yellowish drink is usually consumed in winter, and is served alone rather than during meals.

Sahlep is another traditional Turkish beverage. Sahlep is made from sahlep powder, a mixture of different spices with milk, and sprinkled with cinnamon. Sahlep was served during the Ottoman empire.

Tea is the national hot drink of Turkey. There are two types of tea: the strong tea, koyu cay, and the light tea, acik cay. Turks steep the tea in the teapot for about 15 minutes before serving. When serving koyu cay, two-thirds of the mug is filled with tea and boiling water is added to fill the rest. When serving acik cay, one-third of the mug is filled with tea and boiling water is added to fill the rest. Sugar is added to taste.

Turkish coffee is a very fine, powderlike grind derived from the Arabic bean. Aromatic cardamom is sometimes added to the coffee while it is being ground. Whole cardamom seeds can also be boiled with the coffee and allowed to float to the top when served. The coffee, water, and sugar are boiled together without the use of any filters, so the sludge formed by the coffee is transferred to the cup.

AFIYET OLSUN MEANS "ENJOY YOUR COFFEE!"

In a Turkish home, after a guest has consumed the coffee the cup is turned upside down on the saucer and allowed to cool, and the hostess performs a reading from the coffee grounds remaining in the cup. If called upon, I guess you can always make something up.

As in Egypt, coffee is offered in various degrees of sweetness, and foam is an intrinsic part of a good cup of coffee.

DESSERTS

In Turkey as elsewhere in the Mediterranean, syrup- or honey-soaked pastries are favored— variations on the baklava theme, made with either phyllo dough or shredded wheat and various nuts. Sutlac is Turkish rice pudding, and kazandibi is fried custard. Loukoumia, or Turkish delight, is a gelled sweet often mixed with hazelnuts or pistachios, then cut into cubes and rolled in powdered sugar.

TURKISH RESTAURANTS

Hemsin
39-17 Queens Blvd, Sunnyside
718-482-7998
Subway: No. 7 to 40th St.
Great food in cheery surroundings.
This restaurant is also a bakery.

Turkuaz
95-36 Queens Blvd., Rego Park
718-275-3738
Subway: G, V to 63rd Dr.
This atmospheric spot features
belly dancers on the weekends.

Turkish Grill Restaurant
42-03 Queens Blvd. (42nd St),
Sunnyside
718-786-0206
Subway: No. 7 to 40th St. or 46th
St.

Ayran *(Turkish buttermilk)*

INGREDIENTS

3 cups yogurt

2 cups milk

3 cups iced water

1-1/2 teaspoons salt

DIRECTIONS

Place yogurt in a bowl. Beat with a fork or hand mixer until well blended. Add milk gradually, mixing well. Stir in iced water. Add salt; mix well. Serve cold.

SERVES 6.

Hunkar Begendi *(Sultan's Delight)*

INGREDIENTS

2 onions

2 medium tomatoes or 2
    tablespoons tomato paste

2 tablespoons butter

2 pounds lamb (from shoulder
    or thigh), cubed

1/2 tablespoon black pepper

salt

2-1/2 cups hot water

3 tablespoons butter

2-1/2 tablespoons flour

1-1/2 pounds eggplant

juice of 1 lemon

1 tablespoon salt

1-1/5 cups hot milk

1/4 cup grated kashar cheese
    (Turkish sheep's cheese)

DIRECTIONS

Peel and grate the onions. Peel, seed, and dice the tomatoes. Put 2
tablespoons of butter and grated onions in a large saucepan and sauté over
moderate heat. Add meat and sauté with the onions for 3-4 minutes, until
golden. Cover and cook, stirring occasionally, until the meat absorbs the
water. Season with black pepper and salt. Add the tomatoes or tomato
paste and hot water, and simmer until the meat is tender. Check
occasionally and add water if necessary.

Put 3 tablespoons of butter and flour in a small saucepan, place over
moderate heat, and sauté for 2 minutes, making sure the flour doesn't
brown. Set aside. Grill the eggplants over a gas burner, blackening the
skins. Peel the skins and soak the eggplants in a bowl of water with the
lemon juice for 15 minutes. Remove eggplants and press with your hands
to drain. Cut them into several pieces. Add the eggplant gradually to the
flour, blending well with a fork. Place the saucepan with eggplant and flour
on the stove. Add salt and hot milk, and blend them well by beating
rapidly. Continue beating until the eggplant mixture becomes a dense
paste. Add the grated kashar, stir well, and remove from heat.

When both the kebab and puree are ready, place puree on serving dish,
put the meat decoratively in the middle, and serve hot.

SERVES 6.

Coban *(Shepherd's Salad)*

INGREDIENTS

2 medium cucumbers

7 spring onions

4 medium green peppers

3/4 bunch parsley

7-8 sprigs fresh mint

3 large tomatoes

2 tablespoons lemon juice

1 teaspoon salt

2 tablespoons olive oil

DIRECTIONS

Peel cucumbers and onions. Remove stems and seeds of green peppers. Remove stems of parsley and mint. Chop the onions, green peppers, tomatoes, and cucumbers into a medium dice. Finely chop the mint and parsley. Add lemon juice and salt to olive oil, whisk well, and pour over the salad.

⊙ ARMENIA

THERE'S A SMALL ARMENIAN COMMUNITY
in eastern Queens, around Bayside.
Geographically, I'm not sure you'd place Armenia
squarely in the Middle East, but gastronomically
it fits. Picture what the Turks would be eating if
they were Christians—many of the same foods,
but with the inclusion of pork. The other
influence evident from Armenia's Russian
neighbors is sour cream.

Armenians eat bread with almost everything, and the two traditional types of bread in Armenia are lavash and matnakash. Lavash is a particular favorite of mine—flat bread rolled into circles and prepared in earthenware ovens in the ground (tonirs). Lavash is used to wrap Armenian cheese or meat spiced with onions, greens, and pepper, and marinated before barbecuing over fire or in a tonir. Puffy matnakash is similar to ekmek. Khoravadz is served with fried tomatoes, eggplants, and peppers. Armenians also eat a lot of fish, especially trout known as ishkan in Armenian.

Dolma is also popular in Armenia, and there are two types. Summer dolma is meat stuffed into eggplants, pepper, and tomatoes, while normal dolma is meat wrapped in vine or cabbage leaves, and served with matsuin (similar to yogurt) and garlic. Kufte is made in different ways throughout the country, and gavar kufte is made from minced meat spiced with onions and rolled into balls before boiling in water. It's garnished with butter and served in slices.

Khashlama is boiled meat and potatoes, and kebab is spiced minced meat cooked over a fire or in a pan. Spas is a popular soup that consists of egg and flour stirred into matsoun, a sour dairy product similar to yogurt. Bastourma (pastirma in Turkish) is dried slices of lean beef soaked in spicy chaman (a Middle Eastern spice blend). Khash is scraped bovine shins, boiled in unsalted water until the flesh flakes off the bones, served hot with crushed garlic and eaten with lavash that is soaked in the bowl. Khash is a heavy meal that is not to everyone's taste, and is best eaten in the winter, early in the morning, and with a glass of vodka.

BEVERAGES

Armenia is famous for its wine, brandy, and vodka—in fact, it's known as the motherland of viticulture and wine making. Armenia's viticultural history goes back at least to Biblical times, when Noah's ark came to rest on Mount Ararat, a symbol of Armenia. Noah reportedly established the first vineyard in the Ararat Valley. Many of Armenia's brandies proudly display a picture of Mount Ararat on the label, showing the mountain and the fourth-century monastery of Khor Virap, with Armenian brandy grapes growing in the Ararat Valley. Excavations in this area lend strong support to the theory that some of the very earliest systematic wine making did indeed arise here. Not only does Armenia produce an enviable range of red and white wines, but it also produces a wine made from pomegranates said to have remarkable antioxidant properties that vastly surpasses wine made from grapes and its antiviral properties. Get hammered and healthy at the same time—you can't beat that!

Like their Turkish neighbors, Armenians also drink coffee, tea, Armenian coffee (just like Turkish coffee), and tahn, the yogurt drink described earlier.

DESSERTS

Desserts favored by Armenians are virtually indistinguishable from those eaten throughout the Middle East.

RESTAURANTS

Sevan Bakery & Restaurant
216-09 Horace Harding Expwy.
(north side), Bayside
718-281-0004
Access by public transportation is
extremely difficult
Small, pleasantly decorated spot to
sample Armenian fare.

South America

Colombians are the largest South American immigrant group in Queens, followed by Ecuadorians and Peruvians. Their population nexus is around Jackson Heights and Corona. While there are many Queens eateries serving South American food, ranging from hole-in-the-wall dives to restaurants and clubs, it's also worth checking out some of the street food on weekends on Roosevelt Avenue from about 80th to 100th streets. You'll find a row of food trucks parked along Warren Street, which intersects Roosevelt one block east of 95th Street, selling meals and snacks from Ecuador and Peru. Along Roosevelt, look for Colombian arepas, tamales, sausages, roasted jumbo corn, and cut-up fruits from Ecuador and Peru.

⊙ COLOMBIA

COLOMBIAN CUISINE, IN ITS PURE FORM, isn't likely to make it into *Cooking Light* magazine any time soon. It's a tasty but greasy cuisine that is not particularly hot or spicy.

Hot sauce is generally served on the side for the diner to adjust to taste. The meats Colombians serve tend to be fatty, and lard is the shortening of choice. A favorite component of the platos typicos (typical dishes) is chicharrón—fried pork skin. Chicharrón is an uncured inch-thick slab of bacon with slits cut along the non-rind side, allowing it to curl into a C-shape as it fries. It's pretty much pure fat. If you're concerned about cholesterol, fuggedaboudit.

Colombian food is a 24-hour-a-day cuisine. In many parts of Colombia, where afternoon siesta is still observed, business begins about 8 a.m., continues till noon, closes until 2 p.m. or later, and then reopens until 8 or 9 p.m. After a brief period of refreshment after the workday, Colombians might be ready for dinner at, say, 10 or 11 p.m. Many Colombians are party animals who dance the night away until the wee hours. Others have adapted the mainstream American schedule (at least during the workweek).

This lifestyle is particularly striking should you find yourself on Roosevelt Avenue in Jackson Heights in the wee small hours. Unlike my own neighborhood, at 3 a.m. (especially on a weekend night), stores here are open, and people—in some cases even very young children—are out and about.

The happy result of this spectrum of scheduling is that breakfast (desayunos) is anytime from dawn to late afternoon. Breakfast foods may be the most appealing aspect of Colombian cuisine. The staple of the Colombian diet, served at all times of day, is the arepa. These versatile grilled corn pancakes are used like bread. There are several types of arepas: white or yellow corn, with or without cheese, arepas de chocolo (made from fresh corn), and arepitas (small hockey-puck-sized). As we purchase a hot dog with sauerkraut, Colombians will buy a Colombian grilled cheese

sandwich—arepas con queso blanco (white cheese) or jamon (ham) or huevo (egg) from standing street carts. These are served on the side as a great dunker for stews, meats, chicken, and fish; toasted in the morning with jam, butter, or an egg; or grilled with cheese, ham, and/or vegetables.

As a first foray into Colombian dining, consider a latish breakfast or brunch. Many Colombian restaurants offer some version of "the works" as a breakfast special, which usually includes eggs scrambled with onions and tomatoes, grilled beef, sausage, refried beans, and an arepa with butter and cheese. For something less substantial, there are several interesting breads worth exploring. Arepas, mentioned earlier, are served with butter and cheese, or soaked in egg and milk-like French toast. Buñeulo is a delicious golden fried cheese bread. Pandebono is an equally delicious baked cheese bread.

If you are skipping the heavier stuff and sticking with the breads, you might be inclined to try avena—an oatmeal shake. It's milky, sweetened oatmeal, blended to a milkshake consistency, often served as an accompaniment to the breads at breakfast. An alternative is Colombian hot chocolate, served with the addition of queso blanco; it is surprisingly good this way. Of course, coffee is practically synonymous with Colombia. The preferred sweetener for coffee and other beverages is panela, raw cane sugar crushed to extract the juice and then boiled to evaporate the water, leaving pure, whole, unrefined, cane sugar.

For a quick and tasty lunch, try an empanada, a cornmeal-crusted turnover either filled with savory meats and/or vegetables, or with fruit. An empanada is typically a luncheon meal, but can be a bite-size hors d'oeuvre, too. It also makes good street food from an outdoor vendor. Sancocho is a stew of potato, yucca, and corn, typically featuring chicken, beef, or fish (depending upon the region). A favorite daily staple of Colombians rich and poor, this one-dish meal makes an excellent lunch, often served with rice, green plantains, and salad. Sancocho de cola is made with oxtails, sancocho de pescado with fish, and sancocho del gallina with a hen. Ajiaco is a soup that combines the culinary art of the Spaniards and the Chibchas (the Indians who lived in current-day Bogotá), and is one version of sancocho. It uses three different potatoes—criolle or yellow finn, white, and new potatoes—as well as corn, peas, and chicken in a rich, creamy chicken stock aromatically flavored with guascas, a Colombian herb that tastes like a blend of thyme, tarragon, and basil. Avocado and capers are typical garnishes.

Colombian tamales are much more substantial than their Mexican cousins. They often come wrapped in banana leaves. Fillings can include beef, raisins, pine nuts, and cinnamon; roasted corn, eggplant, and peppers; or chicken, tomato, and cilantro.

For dinner, ceviche de camaron (shrimp ceviche) is an ideal first course. While not strictly Colombian, it's commonly found in American Colombian restaurants. Late 15th-century Spanish explorers found many new and delicious foods in the Americas, but they were quick to import Old World plants and fruit trees, including Seville orange seedlings and lemon seedlings. When native cooks paired these citrus fruits with South America's seafood, one of the world's greatest culinary achievements was born. Ceviche was created when citrus juices were added to fresh raw seafood. The citrus juices not only flavor the fish and shellfish, the acid in the juice "cooks" the seafood, rendering it firm and opaque. Zesty with minced hot chilies, red onion, and fresh cilantro, ceviche is a refreshing and memorable dish.

Most Colombian restaurants offer some version of the plato typico (typical dish). It usually comes with rice, beans, an arepa or arepita, fried plantains, and a variety of meats. If you prefer to zero in on a particular meat, the options for preparation style are usually asada (grilled), frito (fried), a la plancha (prepared on a flat iron piece placed on a grill), or criolle (cooked in a sauce of tomatoes, onions, garlic, and peppers). Most meats are served with a combination of accompaniments that may include rice or French fries, beans, plantains, yucca, salad, and, of course, the ubiquitous arepa.

There are also many excellent Colombian mariscos (seafood) dishes. Cazuela de mariscos is a delicious seafood casserole in a creamy white sauce, sometimes served with coconut rice. Most Colombian restaurants also offer fish and shrimp prepared in ways similar to mainstream American cooking, but with Colombian accompaniments.

DESSERTS

For dessert try arequipe (also called dulce de leche in some Latino countries), an intensely creamy, sugar-crusted, caramel custard that uses sweetened condensed milk as a base. It's often eaten in combination with figs in heavy syrup (brevas en almíbar) and cheese.

BEVERAGES

Colombian beverages are worthy of special note. They range from brown sugar water (aguapanela), Pony Malta (malted soda), Postobon brand fruit-flavored sodas, and natural juices (jugos) and milkshakes (batidas) in a variety of tropical flavors, some of which have no English translations. My favorite flavor of milkshake is lulo (naranjilla), which is sweet and tart and almost indescribable. This fruit became known to North Americans as a beverage at the 1939 New York World's Fair.

Mazamorra is white whole-kernel corn in milk, served with panela or guava paste (bocadillo). It's a Colombian comfort food/drink often consumed before bed.

Beer goes well with Colombian food (just as it does with so many other cuisines). There are many evolved to the degree of subtlety and complexity that some other Latin cuisines have achieved, if you have access to a Colombian restaurant, by all means sample some of its signature dishes.

COLOMBIAN RESTAURANTS

brands of Colombian beer. Cerveza Aguila and Aguila Imperial are two popular labels that are exported to the U.S.

Aguardiente, Colombia's "burning water," is a fiery liquor made from the juice of pressed sugar cane flavored with anise. It has a mean reputation. But canelaso, a popular drink from Bogotá often used as a cold remedy, is a mixture of water, panela, aguardiente, cinnamon, and lime, served warm. It makes a soothing cocktail or nightcap.

Colombian food, on the whole, is simple and hearty. Tropical ingredients give it the distinctively South American flavors that distinguish it from the cuisines of other continents. Characteristics that set it apart from other South American cuisines are the universality of the arepa, the use of potatoes in many dishes, and cream in the sauces. While it hasn't

El Gran Pan De Queso
101-12 43rd Ave., Corona
718-397-9655
Subway: No. 7 to 103rd St., Corona
This small, no-frills ethnic restaurant offers platos typicos and Tolimense (from the Tolima region) selections like a very substantial tamal Tolimense. It also makes four varieties of arepas, which it packages and sells to Latino markets.

La Hacienda Restaurant
86-20 37th Ave., Jackson Heights
718-651-3393, 718-651-0200
Subway: No. 7 to 82nd or 90th St.
Decorated to resemble a Colombian ranch, hence the name. Go on a Tuesday if you want to try ajiaco.

Natives

82-22 Northern Blvd., Jackson
Heights
718-335-0780
Subway: No. 7 to 82nd St.
This converted theater offers a
festive flair and entertainment on
the weekends; try the Seafood
Casserole with Coconut Rice. It's
open 24/7 and does a great
breakfast.

Tierras Colombianas (2 locations)

33-01 Broadway, Astoria
718-956-3012
Subway: R to Steinway St.; N to
Broadway, Flushing
and
82-18 Roosevelt Ave., Jackson
Heights
718-426-8868
Subway: No. 7 to 82nd St.
Good hearty Colombian food.
Pleasant atmosphere. Generous
portions.

Chibcha

79-05 Roosevelt Ave., Jackson
Heights
718-429-9033
Subway: No. 7 to 82nd St.
Although it bills itself as a
restaurant and night club, and
serves Colombian food, food isn't
really Chibcha's thing. It's really a
late night scene. Don't even think
of arriving before 11 p.m. Eat
somewhere else first, and then
come here to drink, dance, and
party hearty. Stop by the Arepa
Lady coming or going.

The Arepa Lady

Corner of Roosevelt Ave. and 79th
Street, Jackson Heights
Subway: No. 7 to 82nd St.
Friday and Saturday nights only
The Arepa Lady is not a restaurant
but a street vendor named Maria
Piedad Cano, or Piedad to her
friends. She sells arepas on Friday
and Saturday nights from about 11
p.m. Her sought-after arepas are so
famous that a story was written
about her in the *New York Times*,
which disclosed the interesting
detail that back in her native
Colombia she was a judge.

Arepas

INGREDIENTS

2 cups milk

4 tablespoons (1/2 stick)
unsalted butter, cut into
pieces, plus more for serving

1-1/2 cups white arepa flour (called
masarepa or arepaharina),
available at Hispanic markets

1 teaspoon salt

1-1/2 tablespoons sugar

1 cup grated processed mozzarella
cheese (do not use fresh
Italian mozzarella)

vegetable oil for the griddle

1-1/4 cups finely grated queso
blanco (Hispanic white
cheese), for serving

DIRECTIONS

In a small saucepan, bring 1-1/2 cups of the milk to a boil. Strain into a bowl and add the butter. Let stand. In a large bowl, stir together the masarepa, salt, sugar, and mozzarella. Make a well in the center and pour in the hot milk. Stir the masarepa mixture and milk together until there are no lumps. Knead the mixture, sprinkling in the remaining 1/2 cup milk, until you have a smooth, sticky dough. This should take about 5 minutes.

Roll the dough into a 1/2-inch-thick sheet between two pieces of wax paper. With a cookie cutter or the rim of a glass, cut out 3-inch circles. Reroll the scraps and cut out more circles. You should have 8. Brush a griddle or large cast-iron skillet lightly with oil and preheat over medium-low heat. Fry as many arepas as will fit until they are soft within and golden and slightly crusty on the outside, about 4 minutes per side. Keep separating the arepas from the skillet with a metal spatula or they will stick. Keep the finished arepas warm in a low oven. To serve, spear a pat of butter with a fork and brush the arepas while still hot. Sprinkle immediately with a generous coating of grated cheese.

MAKES 8 AREPAS.

Ajiaco *(Bogotá's chicken and potato soup)*

INGREDIENTS

2 chicken breasts

2 tablespoons chopped garlic

1 medium chopped onion

salt, to taste

8 medium baking potatoes, peeled
  and cut into slices

2 cubes of chicken bouillon

1 bunch scallions

1 bunch cilantro

12 small yellow potatoes, halved

3-4 tablespoons dried guascas
  (found in Latin markets—a
  must for this dish)

2 ears of corn, cut in halves

1 can of Papas Crioles (pickled
  potatoes found in Latin
  markets)

1 cup of heavy cream

2 tablespoons capers

2 avocados, peeled, pitted, and
  thinly sliced

DIRECTIONS

The night before, marinate the chicken breasts in garlic, onion, and salt.
The next day, cover the breasts with water in a heavy casserole and cook
until tender. Remove chicken skin and slice breasts into strips. Reserve the
stock.

Cook the baking potatoes in the reserved stock until they start to
disintegrate. Add salt to taste, bouillon cubes, extra water as necessary,
scallions, cilantro, yellow potatoes, guascas, corn, and rinsed canned papas
crioles. When cooked, remove cilantro and scallions. Pour the chicken stock
over the chicken in large soup bowls. Add 3 tablespoons of cream, a
teaspoon of capers, and sliced avocado to each bowl.

SERVES 4.

Tostones

INGREDIENTS

vegetable oil for frying

3-4 green plantains, sliced 1 inch thick and then peeled

3 cloves of crushed garlic in a bowl of warm salted water

DIRECTIONS

Heat oil in a large skillet. Fry the plantain slices, a few at a time so as not to crowd, about 3 minutes on each side, removing the done ones to a paper towel to drain. When they're cool enough to handle, flatten each slice to about 1/4 inch using a spatula, your hand, a tortilla press, or the bottom of a heavy pot—whatever works for you. Dip each flattened slice into the water with the garlic and then drain well on paper towels. Reheat the oil, adding more if needed so that it's about 1/2 inch deep. Fry the plantain patties for about 3 minutes on each side until golden. Serve immediately with salt.

Arequipe

INGREDIENTS

½ gallon whole milk

2 pounds sugar

pinch of salt

pinch of baking soda

1 stick cinnamon

1 long green onion (optional)

DIRECTIONS

Heat milk, sugar, salt, and baking soda over medium-high heat in a large, heavy-bottomed pot—preferably one made of copper—and mix until sugar is dissolved. Add cinnamon and onion. Without stirring, bring all ingredients to a boil. Lower heat and cook, stirring occasionally with a wooden spoon, for 1 to 1-½ hours or until sauce turns to a caramel color and thickens.

⊙ PERU/ECUADOR

PERUVIAN CUISINE APPEARS TO BE IN THE throes of making the transition from a strictly ethnic cuisine to one that's more widely known and appreciated by mainstream Americans.

The giveaway is that Peruvian eateries are popping up in non-Peruvian neighborhoods. The Peruvian specialty driving this craze is rotisserie chicken, or pollos a la brasa, chicken that's been marinated in Peruvian spices. This dish is growing in popularity as both an eat-in and take-out food. Peruvian hasn't reached the level of ubiquity of, say, Thai food, but given time, more and more diners will be seeking this delicious and varied cuisine.

Unsurprisingly, given the geographic similarity and proximity of Peru and Ecuador, the food is similar. Ecuadorian restaurants aren't emerging the way Peruvian restaurants are; the ones I've sampled seem to offer more pan-Latino fare than anything uniquely Ecuadorian.

Criollo is the word Peruvians use for their traditional food. The primary ingredients found in nearly every Peruvian dish are rice, potatoes, chicken, pork, lamb, and fish. Most of these meals include one of the different kinds of aji, or Peruvian hot peppers: yellow aji pepper, red aji pepper, and red rocoto pepper.

The diet of the pre-Colombian Quechan communities of the Andes relied heavily on the potato, the basic element in soups, stews, and pachamanca—a mixture of meats and vegetables cooked with hot stones in a covered pit in the ground. Leftover potatoes from the pachamanca were put out to dry. When the bits were rehydrated and cooked in a stew, they became carapulca (from the Quechua kala, meaning "hot stone," and purka,

PERUVIAN STREET FOOD ON ROOSEVELT AVENUE

meaning "hole in the ground"), eaten throughout the country to this day.

According to the International Potato Center in Lima, the Incas cultivated more than 1,000 varieties of potato. Pizarro and his Spanish conquistadores introduced the potato to Europe in the 1600s, bringing back in exchange beef, chicken, pork, and lamb. These domesticated animals were added to a diet of game including llama, guinea pig, wild hare, and various types of fowl.

Papa a la huancaina, an entrée from the Andean highlands, is potatoes covered with a spicy sauce made from cheese, milk, aji, and peanuts, and garnished with black olives, hard-boiled egg, and lettuce. Lomo saltado, or diced meat (beef or pork) sautéed with onions and peppers, is another highlands favorite, usually accompanied by rice and a few French fries. (Peruvians see no redundancy in eating potatoes and rice.) For a delicious snack, sometimes available from food trucks, try papa rellena, a potato stuffed with vegetables and fried. Parihuela, a fragrant seafood soup, and chupe de camarones, a creamy shrimp soup with vegetables and a fried egg, are both prepared with an aji stock

> **PERUVIANS CONSUME AN ESTIMATED 65 MILLION CUY (GUINEA PIGS) EACH YEAR.** This dining experience requires patience to pick scant, sinewy meat from a bony carcass—often with the head staring up from the plate. I've yet to spot cuy on any menu, but have seen it frozen in the meat cases of Latino markets and have heard it's sometimes available from street vendors. No worse than eating rabbit, I suppose.

characteristic of the coastal cuisine.

Peruvian cuisine is extremely cosmopolitan. The food reveals not only a Spanish influence but the influence of many waves of European and Asian immigration. Between 1849 and 1874, 100,000 Chinese immigrants arrived in Peru. As a result, Peru is by far the Latin American country with the most Chinese restaurants, supporting more than 2,000 chifas, or Chinese restaurants.

Lomo saltado is not only a classic Peruvian dish but a typical Sino-Peruvian fusion. The Chinese stir-frying techniques brought over in the last half of the 19th century put Peruvian aji into the same pan with ginger and soy sauce for the first time.

Peruvians claim that ceviche originated in Peru, although it is eaten all over Latin America. Tiraditos, a cousin of ceviche, demonstrates the Japanese influence on Peruvian cuisine. Instead of the fish being chopped before being marinated in citrus, it is sliced into thin sashimilike strips. Other Asian-inspired favorites are jalea (deep-fried mixed fish and shellfish) and coctel de camarones (shrimp cocktail).

In a Peruvian restaurant, you can also expect to find criollo specialties like arroz con pato (duck cooked with rice), cau cau (tripe and vegetable stew), and anticuchos (barbecued pieces of meat, chicken, or fish on a skewer). Ocopa, the signature sauce from the southern city of Arequipa, is a mixture of ground pre-Columbian peanuts and aji, with the addition of dairy products introduced by the Spaniards. Tacu tacu de pescado (fish filet with Peruvian-style rice and bean risotto) is a specialty of Lima. Chicharron to a Peruvian means marinated roast pork. The word is the same as the one for Colombian fried pork skin, but that's where the resemblance ends.

DESSERTS

Desserts include delicacies like arroz con leche (rice pudding), mazamorra morada (a purple colored corn pudding), suspiros a la limeña (a sticky-sweet pudding), picarones (deep-fried pumpkin and sweet potato doughnuts dipped in sugar cane syrup), and turrón de Doña Pepa (a multicolored cake).

BEVERAGES

Pisco is a colorless brandy or spirit made from grapes. It is very high in alcohol, and traditionally comes from southern Peru. Begin your Peruvian dinner with a Pisco sour, the nation's signature cocktail. Sangria is also poplular in Peru, and comes in a pitcher with small cubes of apple floating in it. Chica de jora is a fermented corn drink equivalent to beer. The two main beers are Cristal and Pilsen.

Chica morada is a sort of nonalcoholic corn punch served like sangria with bits of apple.

Like the Colombians, Peruvians also enjoy batidos de frutas con leche o agua (fruit shakes with milk or water). The soda of choice is Inca Cola, which tastes vaguely like a sweet Pepsi and is chartreuse in color. South Americans regard soft drinks that come out of a spigot with suspicion, and are loyal to the bottled brands that come from home.

The incipient trendiness of Peruvian cuisine is not without good reason. Its flavors are varied, complex, and sophisticated. It you haven't yet sampled Peruvian food, what are you waiting for?

PERUVIAN RESTAURANTS

Inti Raymi

86-14 37th Ave, Jackson Heights
718-424-1938
Subway: No. 7 to 82nd St. or 90th St.
Named after the Peruvian holiday that pays homage to the sun god, an important god in Incan culture. A full-service Peruvian restaurant that serves Peruvian breakfast on weekend mornings. Don't miss its papas rellenas.

La Pollada de Laura

102-03 Northern Blvd., Corona
718-426-7818
Subway: No. 7 to 103rd St.
Killer ceviche, way cheap prices.

Punta Sal

100-05 Metropolitan Ave., Forest Hills

718-896-1001

Subway: E, F, V, R to 71st-Continental; Q 23 to Metropolitan Ave.

The forte here is Peru's coastal cuisine, but this restaurant offers a range of dishes from throughout Peru.

El Anzuelo Fino Restaurant (2 locations)

25-39 Steinway St., Astoria

718-204 7711

Subway: G, V, R to Steinway St.

and

98-01 Jamaica Ave., Woodhaven

718-846-0909

Subway: J (Z at rush hours) to Woodhaven Blvd.

Full range of traditional Peruvian food. The Astoria location is more attractive than the Woodhaven one.

Pio Pio (2 locations)

84-13 Northern Blvd., Jackson Heights

718-426-1010

Subway: No. 7 to 82nd St.

and

62-30 Woodhaven Blvd., Rego Park

718-458-0606

Subway: V, R, G to Woodhaven Blvd./Slattery Plaza, then Q 11, 53

bus along Woodhaven Blvd (south)

The rotisserie chicken is the big deal here. The Jackson Heights location has style and pizzazz. The Rego Park location is much smaller and less well decorated. The food is the same.

ECUADORIAN RESTAURANTS

Alfa Y Omega

40-18 108th St., Corona

718-476-9805 or 718-779-8142

Subway: No. 7 to 111th St.

Small, cozy, family-run place.

El Dorado Café

102-02 Roosevelt Ave., Corona

718-426-5992

Subway: No. 7 to 103rd St.

Ceviche

INGREDIENTS

1 pound of firm white fish fillets (snapper, monkfish, etc.)

1 large red onion, finely sliced

1 heaping teaspoon salt

1 or 2 fresh aji amarillo (yellow Peruvian chilies), seeded, and finely chopped; you can substitute canned aji (or tabasco sauce if aji peppers are unavailable)

3/4 cup of fresh lime or lemon juice (preferably key limes or Mexican lemons)

fresh lettuce leaves

2 tablespoons fresh coriander, chopped

4 ears of corn, cooked and cut into 2-inch pieces

1 pound sweet potatoes, roasted in the skin, peeled, and sliced into 1/2-inch-thick rounds

1 pound yucca, peeled, cut into little-finger-sized slices, and boiled until soft

DIRECTIONS

Rinse the fish thoroughly under cold water. Cut fish into small cubes and place in a large bowl. Finely slice the red onion and combine with the fish. Add salt, aji pepper, or Tabasco sauce to taste. Mix well. Pour the lime or lemon juice over the fish—enough to cover it completely. Cover the bowl with plastic wrap and refrigerate for 1 to 1 1/2 hours (up to 8 hours is O.K.). To serve, line each plate with lettuce. Place a mound of ceviche in the center and sprinkle with chopped coriander. Surround it with corn pieces and sweet potato and yucca slices.

SERVES 4-6.

Pisco Sour

INGREDIENTS
crushed ice

1-1/2 tablespoons lime or lemon juice (about half a large lemon)

1 teaspoon superfine sugar

3 tablespoons of Pisco

a dash of bitters

DIRECTIONS
Half-fill a small glass with crushed ice. Squeeze the lime or lemon juice directly into the glass and drop in the fruit. Add the sugar and stir until dissolved. Pour in the Pisco and stir. A dash of bitters may be added if desired.

SERVES 1.

Aji de Gallina

INGREDIENTS

4-1/2-pound chicken, boiled in 1 quart of water with 1 leek, 1 carrot, 1 onion, and salt until meat is easily removed from bones (about 1-1/2 to 2 hours)

1 onion, finely chopped

1 clove garlic, crushed

1/2 teaspoon cumin seeds

3/4 cup vegetable oil

2 cups soft bread crumbs, soaked in 1 cup evaporated milk

3 tablespoons blended hot Peruvian pepper (aji)

1 cup grated cheese

1/2 cup walnuts, chopped

2 pounds boiled, peeled, yellow potatoes

optional garnishes: black olives, slices of hard-boiled egg

DIRECTIONS

Remove chicken meat from bones and shred, reserving stock. Brown onions, garlic, and cumin seeds in 1/2 cup oil. Add soaked bread crumbs and simmer 15 minutes. Blend onion/crumb mixture in blender or food processor for creamier sauce.

Fry hot pepper in remaining 1/4 cup oil, then add it to mixture together with chicken, cheese, and walnuts. Simmer 10 minutes, thinning with chicken stock and adding salt as necessary. Sauce should be fairly thick. Pour sauce over bed of potatoes and serve with rice. Garnish with black olive and slices of hard-boiled egg.

SERVES 6.

Colombia, Ecuador, and Peru make up the lion's share of the South American population of Queens. Two other countries, Argentina and Brazil, contribute a minute fraction of the total, but their cuisines are so distinctive and delicious that they shouldn't be neglected.

⊙ ARGENTINA

UNLIKE COLOMBIA, ECUADOR, OR PERU, THE population of Argentina is more European than mestizo (European/Indian) or Indian.

Italian and Spanish settlers have influenced Argentinean cuisine a great deal, and the French, Germans, Swiss, and Eastern Europeans have left their culinary stamp as well. Argentina was never a heavily populated area; as a result, it claims almost no indigenous cuisine before the arrival of European immigrants.

Most Argentincans eat four meals a day. Desayuno (breakfast) is a light meal of rolls and jam with coffee. For almuerzo (lunch), many Argentineans eat meat and vegetables or salads. After work but before dinner, people go to confiterías (cafés) to drink espresso and eat picadas, small dishes of cheese, mussels, salami, anchovies, olives, and peanuts. Cena (dinner) in the evening is the largest meal of the day and almost always includes beef.

Argentina has its own version of the empanada. These half-moon-shaped pastries are filled with meats, vegetables, cheeses, and spices. The most popular variety contains ground beef, olives, hard-boiled eggs, tomatoes, and spices. Another popular one is the humita, which is filled with a creamy mixture of corn, cheese, nutmeg, and thick white sauce. Empanadas are sold in bakeries, and some restaurants serve small versions as appetizers.

If there is a single food that represents Argentina, it is beef. Argentineans are carnivores to the max. The pampas, Argentina's rich grassland plains, rest in the shadows of the Andes. They provide good

TRADITIONAL ARGENTINE DANCE PERFORMED BY LAURA AND PABLO OF BALLET LOS PAMPAS AT TANGO MAMBO IN FOREST HILLS

land for growing wheat and corn and grazing land for cattle and sheep. Grass-fed Argentine beef is highly prized for its flavor and tenderness.

Cattle were introduced to Argentina in the 16th century. Less than 200 years later they were running wild in vast herds. As in the U.S., the romantic image of the gaucho, or cowboy, pervades Argentina's culture. Unfortunately, because of issues of hoof-and-mouth disease, the FDA has banned imports of Argentine beef.

Argentine barbecue is known as asado. Asado consists of various meats and sausages cooked on a grill called a parillada over wooden coals. Side dishes may include salads and French-fried potatoes, with a good red wine being the beverage of choice. Asado is not authentic without a delicious marinade called chimichuri, a melange of olive oil, vinegar, and finely chopped parsley, oregano, onion, and garlic, all seasoned with salt, cayenne, and black pepper. Chimichuri is used as both a marinade and a sauce served along with grilled meats.

Argentina, like the U.S., is a country of immigrants, mainly from Europe. In the early part of the 20th century there was a large wave of immigrants from Italy, and today almost 40 percent of Argentineans are of Italian descent. According to a Colombian friend of mine, people from Argentina speak Spanish with an Italian accent. So I guess pasta is as Argentinean as pizza and bagels are American.

Argentinean Italian food is very rich and uses cream in many of its dishes. Noquis, the Argentine version of gnocchi (Italian potato dumplings), are a popular favorite. Milanesa Napolitana is an "Italian" dish invented in Argentina. It's a breaded veal cutlet with a slice of cheese and ham covered with tomato sauce and put in the oven until the cheese melts. The owner of the Napoli restaurant in Buenos Aires created it by mistake. A lucky mistake.

DESSERT

Argentineans make some great desserts. Dulce de leche—sweetened caramelized milk—a favorite throughout Latin America, is a matter of national pride in Argentina. Any Argentinean will tell you that his or her country makes it best.

Alfajors consist of thick dulce de leche sandwiched between two cookie wafers that are coated with either chocolate or a sugary glaze. These tasty cookie-type treats are a mainstay of Argentine snacking. Panqueque de manzana (apple crepes) is another delicious dessert.

BEVERAGES

Maté is widely considered the national beverage in Argentina. Yerba (flex paraguariensis) is an evergreen member of the holly family that grows wild in Argentina, Brazil, Chile, and Peru, and is most abundant in Paraguay where it is also cultivated. Gram for gram, yerba maté has less caffeine than either coffee or tea, yet contains antioxidants and a variety of vitamins, minerals, and amino acids that boost energy, fight fatigue, and help lower cholesterol.

To properly prepare maté, you need yerba leaves, a maté, and a bombilla. A maté is the container, usually a gourd or wooden cup, where the yerba is placed. The bombilla is a metal straw used to ingest the tea. The uninitiated might find this tea extremely strong and bitter, but after a few attempts there is something about it that brings you back for more. Yerba leaves are known for their high caffeine and medicinal value, and maté is claimed to be the best remedy for digestive problems.

Soft drinks and fruit juices are popular in Argentina. Licuados are milky fruit shakes called batidas elsewhere in South America. Chocolate is often served at breakfast. Argentineans also drink coffee, usually espresso. Café chico is a small cup of strong, black coffee. Café cortado is a small coffee with a little milk, often in a glass. Café con leche, coffee with lots of milk, is usually served only at breakfast.

Argentina is the fifth-largest wine producer in the world, but its citizens drink so much of this excellent wine that until recently, not much was exported. Mendoza, at the foot of the Andes, is the epicenter of the Argentine wine industry. Mendoza's population is primarily of Italian descent, perhaps accounting for their way with wine.

ARGENTINE RESTAURANTS

La Fusta
80-32 Baxter Ave., Jackson Heights
718-429-8222
Subway: No. 7 to 82nd St.
Argentine steak house.

La Porteña Restaurant
74-25 37th Ave., Jackson Heights
718-458-8111
Subway: No. 7 to 82nd St.
Argentine barbecue. Proteña is a name for a resident of Buenos Aires.

La Cabaña Argentina
95-51 Roosevelt Ave., Jackson Heights
718-429-4388
Subway: No. 7 to 90th St.
Argentine meats and cuisine.

Tango Mambo
111-08 Queens Blvd. (off 75th Ave.), Forest Hills
718-520-6488
Subway: E, F to 75th Ave.
Owned by an Argentinean couple who are also performers. Live music and tango exhibitions on weekends.

El Farolito
25-39 Steinway St.
718-204-7711
Subway: G, V, R to Steinway St.

Chimichuri Sauce

There are many variations on this condiment, which is served by Argentineans with everything from empanadas to grilled steak. Mince the ingredients by hand or with a food processor.

INGREDIENTS

½ cup olive oil

2 tablespoons fresh lemon juice

⅓ cup minced fresh parsley

1 clove garlic

2 minced shallots

1 teaspoon minced basil, thyme, or oregano, or mixture

salt and pepper to taste

DIRECTIONS

Combine all ingredients. Let sit for at least 2 hours before serving.

Dulce de Leche *(Milk jam)*

The easy way to make dulce de leche.

INGREDIENTS

1 can sweetened condensed milk
large pot with metal rack

DIRECTIONS

Place the can inside the pot on top of the rack. Add water until it reaches about 2 inches above top of can. Bring water to a boil and simmer for 4 hours, checking periodically to make sure the can is always completely covered with water. Failure to keep the can covered with water can lead to an explosion! Let the can to cool several hours until it can be handled comfortably. Open it and serve the golden-brown confection over flan, as a filling for crepes or cakes, or just plain. For breakfast it can be spread it on croissants, rolls, or toast!

Carbonada Criolla

(Argentine vegetable beef stew)

INGREDIENTS

3 tablespoons vegetable oil

2 garlic cloves, halved

2 onions, finely chopped

1 pound stewing steak, cubed

2 ears of corn, cut into 1-inch slices

$1/2$ pound pumpkin, peeled and cubed

$1/2$ pound potatoes, peeled and cubed

3 cups beef stock

$1/2$ pound long-grain rice

2 tomatoes, chopped

1 tablespoon freshly chopped parsley

2 green bell peppers, chopped

salt and pepper to taste

DIRECTIONS

Heat the oil in a large saucepan. Add the garlic and onion and sauté until softened. Add the beef and brown on all sides. Add the remaining ingredients and mix well. Bring to a boil, then reduce the heat, cover, and simmer for $1-1/2$ to 2 hours, or until the meat is tender, adding more stock or water to cover meat as necessary. Correct seasonings with additional salt and pepper to taste. Serve hot.

SERVES 4.

⦿ BRAZIL

QUEENS'S BRAZILIAN POPULATION IS SO small that it doesn't show up on the 2000 census, but I know they're here. There are two giveaways: I've gone to Brazilian restaurants in Queens and been surrounded by multiethnic tables of people speaking Portuguese. The other giveaway is a few outrageously sexy lingerie stores catering to Brazilians. Brazilian women love their scanty panties.

In South America, a continent of multiculturalism, Brazil is a contender for the most diverse. Brazilian cuisine is an amalgam of the cooking heritage of three groups: the native Indians, the conquering Portuguese, and the African slaves they brought to work in the sugarcane fields.

The Indian influence is particularly strong in the north, and is expressed culinarily by the presence of various fruits, nuts, greens, and herbs. One characteristic dish is pato no tukupi, duck with an herb sauce that numbs the tongue. Manioca, or cassava root, is a major starch in Brazil and the source of farofa, a bread-crumblike condiment unique to the Brazilian table. And guaraná is a tropical berry that's used in a popular Brazilian soft drink. The only edible part of the guaraná fruit is the black seed packed deep inside. The most common use for guaraná is in soft-drink production. Since the seeds contain high levels of caffeine, the beverages produced with guaraná are great for an energy boost. In the United States, it's used in Red Bull.

The Portuguese arrived in Brazil in the 1500s and rapidly imposed not just their language but also their cuisine. Examples of Portuguese influence on Brazilian cooking include bacalhao (salt cod) and empadinhos, the Brazilian take on empanadas.

The Portuguese set up large plantations in the state of Bahia on the central coast. Bahia is in some ways reminiscent of the American South, and this is where Afro-Brazilian soul food is found. Vatapá (spicy fish or shrimp paste soup with coconut milk) and muqueca (Brazilian fish, tomato, and coconut milk stew) are famous Bahian dishes. The use of coconut milk and dendê palm oil derives from African cuisine, although Brazilian dendê is lighter than African dendê.

Brazilians eat a light breakfast. Lunch, or almoco, is the main meal of the day, and is served from about 11:30 a.m. to 3 p.m. Dinner, or jantar, is eaten late and usually consists of light and simple fare. Cafezinho, otherwise known as

espresso, is drunk throughout the day.

Brazilian restaurants in Queens have adapted to a more American schedule.

In Portuguese, appetizers are called salgadinhos. Coxinha is one of Brazil's tasty triumphs in that category. It's a common dish in Brazil that's often available as a street food. Spiced chicken is rolled in mashed manioc or potatoes and fried into a drumstick-shaped dumpling. Farofa, a common side dish in Brazil, is basically cassava flour toasted with butter. Various ingredients can be added, or it can be used as a stuffing.

Feijoada is considered by most to be the national dish of Brazil. Versions of this black bean stew vary, depending on the types of meats and sausages added into it. Many Brazilians eat this thick, filling stew as a side dish or a meal itself. Salpicao—which translates as "shoestring salad"—is another of the many popular side dishes served in Brazilian cuisine. This salad mainly consists of chicken, hearts of palm, potato sticks, peas, apples, and mayonnaise.

In the early 1900s, German and Italian immigrants settled in southern Brazil in the area known as the pampas, or high plains, and began raising livestock and farming the land. To celebrate the harvest, they began a tradition of feasts that included fresh fruits and vegetables prepared and served at a communal table. Tantalizing cuts of beef, chicken, pork, and fish would be seasoned and barbecued on skewers over open fire pits by the gauchos (ranchers). Everyone would eat their fill.

Restaurants called churrascarias, inspired by the food at these feasts, have spread throughout Brazil. The word churrascaria derives from Portuguese, and it literally means "house of barbecue." The European Brazilians elaborated the idea further around the turn of the century, and it has become synonymous for a place in which you continuously partake of all kind of meats until you are more than fully satiated. This system is called rodízio, which means "in cycle" for the waiters who circle the premises with the meat.

There are three churrascarias in Queens. The oldest of the three, Green Field, was opened by a Korean owner who discovered the cuisine in Brazil. In this bastion of multiculturalism, Green Field stands out as having the most diverse parties of diners at its tables. You will see Asians, whites, and blacks enjoying one another's company and the food. Maybe they're all Brazilians. Maybe not.

The food itself is a little like the Sizzler on steroids. There's a vast buffet bar of vegetables, fruits, salads, and side dishes of all descriptions. Back at your table after loading up, you'll notice a hockey puck on your table that is reddish on one side and green on the other. A green hockey puck means "bring me some meat!" A parade of servers cruise by the tables bearing enormous skewers of a wide assortment of meats, offering it to the green hockey-pucked tables. When you've eaten your fill (or are just resting), flip your puck to the red to indicate "uncle."

Churrascarias may not be the last word in fine dining, but they are very festive, often with live music, and there is no way to leave hungry.

DESSERTS

Rich, sweet desserts made with eggs and sugar were introduced by the Portuguese colonists. Custard and flan are popular desserts (sobremesas). They're made from flour, eggs, and orange juice or coconut milk, and are flavored with nuts, caramel, coffee, cheese, prunes, lemon, or other fruits. Pudding is also a favorite, and comes in many flavors—corn, coconut, bread, milk, fruit, and manioc. Other popular desserts are docinhos (homemade bonbons), guava or other fruit paste with catupiri cheese, chilled avocado cream, and pumpkin, lime pies, fried bananas, and orange slices. Sweet sauces made with fruits like prune, pineapple, mango, guava, and passion fruit top desserts, ice creams, and puddings.

Candies in different colors and shapes, like cocadas (coconut candies) and pumpkin candies, are common treats at festas and as munchies on street corners. Some have amusingly evocative names: urchin's foot (peanut brittle), two loves (sweet shredded coconut), little kisses (cherry rolls), she and I (made with cocoa and condensed milk and rolled in chocolate), and mother-in-law's eyes (stuffed prunes). Tropical fruits are abundant in Brazil. Passion fruit mousse is a favorite dessert in Queens's Brazilian eateries.

BEVERAGES

Brazilians drink chilled sweetened fruit juices (sucos), soft drinks (refrigerantes), and beer. Sugarcane juice, caldo de cana, is taken with savory nibblers. Coconut water is a favorite, while refreshing and sweet guaraná soda is popular all over. When milk is added to blended fresh fruits instead of water, sucos then become vitaminas. Cachaça (sugarcane liquor, also known as aguardente de cana, pinga, and other names), the national spirit of Brazil, has an alcoholic strength of 38 percent to 54 percent by volume. Caipirinha, considered Brazil's national drink, consists of cachaça, fresh lime juice, and sugar over ice. Batidas are mixes of cachaça, fruit juices, and sugar.

Brazil is the biggest producer of coffee (arabica and robusta) in the world. Its coffee is medium-bodied, clear, sweet, and low-acid. Brazilians take coffee in many ways—black, with hot milk (cafe con leite), cream, or vanilla ice cream, sweet or iced. Coffee Brazilian-style, cafezinho, is strong and black, sweetened with sugar, and served in a demitasse.

Tea (cha) varieties include guaraná and cha maté, the same yerba maté drink enjoyed by Argentineans.

BRAZILIAN RESTAURANTS

Sabor Tropical
36-18 30th Ave., Astoria
718-777-8506
Subway: N to 30th Ave.
A cheerfully inviting place with
excellent, authentic Brazilian food.
Try its coxinha de galinha to begin.

Malagueta
25-35 36th Ave. (at 28th Street),
Long Island City
718-937-4821
Subway: N, W to 36th Ave.
A more upscale Brazilian eatery.
Excellent moqueca de camarão
(shrimp stew with coconut).
Feijoada served on Saturdays only.

Brasil Coffee House
48-19 Vernon Blvd., Hunters Point
(Long Island City)
718-729-5969
Subway: No. 7 to Vernon Blvd.-
Jackson Ave.
The Brasil Coffee House is an
offshoot of a Brazilian coffee
importer. It serves the perfect cup
of coffee and Brazilian snacks.

CHURRASCARIAS

Green Field Churrascaria
108-01 Northern Blvd. (at 108th
St.), Corona
718-672-5202
Subway: No. 7 to 111th St.
This original Queens churrascaria
now has several branches
throughout the U.S. Bring your
appetite.

Master Grill
34-09 College Point Blvd., College
Point
718-762-0300
Subway: No. 7 to Main St.; walk
north (10 min.) to College Point
Blvd.
An over-the-top exterior of
multicolor striped minarets houses
this churrascaria with seating for
1,000.

Churrascaria Tropical
36-08 30th Ave., Astoria
718-777-8171
Subway: N to 30th Ave.
The smallest and possibly the best
of the churrascarias in Queens.

Feijoada

INGREDIENTS

1 can of black beans (15.5 ounces)
2 tablespoons vegetable oil
4 cloves garlic, chopped
salt and ground black pepper
1 large onion, chopped
4 bay leaves
1 teaspoon dried oregano
1 pound of pork tenderloin
6 ounces slab bacon, diced
1/2 pound smoked pork sausages, sliced
1/2 pound hot Portuguese sausage, like linguica, sliced
1/4 pound carne seca (Brazilian salted cured beef), if available
chopped fresh cilantro or parsley

DIRECTIONS

Add black beans to a medium-size pot with oil, salt, half the garlic, chopped onions, bay leaves, oregano, and pepper. Cook for about 15 minutes over medium heat. Set aside. (To make the feijoada creamy, liquefy 1/2 cup of black beans in the blender and return to pot.)

In a separate pan, thoroughly cook cubes of pork tenderloin and bacon with remaining garlic. Add the sliced sausages and carne secca and stir over medium heat until all the liquid is absorbed. Add the cooked meat to the pot with the black beans. Cook your feijoada 10 more minutes to let the meat soak in the black beans. Sprinkle with chopped cilantro or parsley and serve with rice.

SERVES 6-8.

Caipirinha *(Brazil's favorite cocktail)*

INGREDIENTS
1 lime, quartered

1 tablespoon of sugar

½ cup of ice cubes with water

1 shot of cachaça

DIRECTIONS
Place the lime and sugar in the bottom of a tall glass. Using the handle of a wooden spoon, crush and mash the limes. Add the ice and cachaça. Stir well.

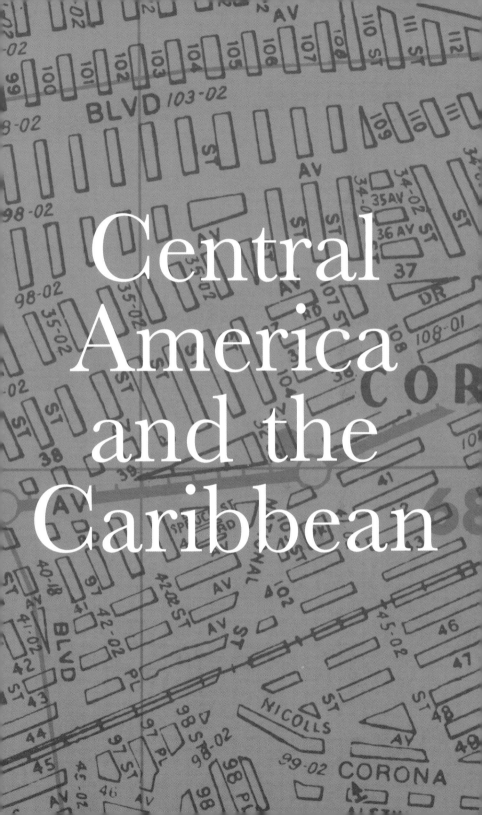

Central America and the Caribbean

⊙ MEXICO

ABOUT A QUARTER OF QUEENS CHEWS
to a Latin beat. Half of those are from Central
America. The most evident and influential of the
Central American cuisines is Mexican. In other
parts of the country, most notably the southwest,
Mexican food has been invading local kitchens for
years.

These cuisines even have names like Tex-Mex or New Mexican. In Queens, large numbers of Mexicans didn't start arriving until about 15 years ago. Between the 1990 census and the 2000 census, Queens's Mexican population tripled to about 38,000. As things stand now, if the Mexicans decided to leave en masse tomorrow, restaurants in New York City, both upscale and modest, would be bereft of staff. The collateral benefit to the stomachs of Queens is that many of the fancy-shmancy restaurants' kitchen help, after learning the business and saving some money, decide to open their own places here, featuring the cuisines of their home.

The cuisines (and I do mean plural) of Mexico are sophisticated and varied. They can be divided into two categories—northern and everywhere else. The one that most of us gringos are familiar with is antojitos Mexicanos, literally "Mexican-style whims." These are the corn and tortilla-based specialties that include dishes like enchiladas, tacos, tamales, quesadillas, chalupas, and tostadas, which evolved directly from the original Indian cooking. In Mexico

MEXICAN DIOS DE LOS MUERTOS BREADS

today, these antojitos Mexicanos serve as inexpensive but delicious staples for those without a lot of money, and are popular with the more affluent as informal snacks or light meals. They're based primarily on the relatively simple cooking of the northern Mexican states of Chihuahua and Nuevo Leon, where most of the early Mexican immigrants to this country emigrated from.

Chilies are what give Mexican food its fiery heat. Chilies, the fruit of several different capsicums, a genus of the nightshade family, are indispensable to Mexican cooking. Used both fresh and dried,

Mexicans can distinguish between the heat and flavor of various varieties. The ancho chili is the most popular, used in moles, salsas, and cut into strips as a garnish, or ground into a seasoning as chili powder. Other popular varieties of chilies are jalapeño, poblano, serrano, guajillo, chipotle, pasilla, habanero (get out your fire extinguisher), ancho, mulatto, and cascabel.

Along with chilies, other ingredients that impart that characteristically Mexican flavor are copious quantities of cilantro, canela—a Mexican spice similar to a mild cinnamon—key lime, and chocolate, used most famously in mole sauce.

Corn, the basic staple of the Mexican diet, is used in flour form for tortillas and tacos, as grits to fill tamales, and as posole—dried kernels treated with lime to remove the outer skin—for stews and soups. Rice is an integral part of Mexican cuisine. It's used in main courses, as a side dish, in desserts, and even in drinks.

The more exotic ingredients include nopales (tender opuntia cactus leaves), cuitaloche (corn fungus with the taste of an earthy truffle), and epazote, a pungent, leafy Mexican herb that's reputed to have the power to stop flatulence.

All kinds of beans are integral to Mexican cuisine. Small beans are often served refrito (refried in lard, tasty but heavy) or de la olla (boiled and served in a light broth).

Mexican cheeses have a unique taste and texture. Different cheeses are used for different purposes. For example, Oaxaca is a melting cheese. Crumbly ranchero is great in tacos. Cotija is another crumbly cheese, more pungent in flavor than ranchero. Panela is a soft cheese.

BREAKFAST

In California and the Southwest, Mexican breakfasts are embraced by the mainstream population, as well they should be. They are tasty, cheap, and that little extra zing of spice wakes you right up. If, by some tragic oversight, you've never tried Mexican food, breakfast could be just the place to start. The classic desayuno Mexicano (Mexican breakfast) is huevos rancheros (ranch-style eggs): an egg over a fried tortilla topped with red or green salsa and some cheese, usually served with rice and refried beans. You might also want to try a side of Mexican chorizo (sausage). Breakfast tacos—a taco filled with eggs and other breakfast-y accompaniments—are the perfect breakfast to grab on the run, if you have a taqueria in your nabe.

LUNCH

In addition to the familiar antojitos Mexicanos, another perfect lunch is a torta. In some countries, the word torta implies "cake," but in Mexico it usually means sandwich—a very hearty sandwich filled with a mixture of meat, cheeses, beans, and sauces in various combinations. Mexicans use a bread made especially for this—bolillo or telera. A cemita is a Pueblan variant of the torta, which takes its name from its oversized, slightly sweet sesame seed bun.

You can find all of the above at all of Queens's Mexican restaurants. After all, it's the working classes that are emigrating here to find work. However, the largest segment of Queens's Mexican expats come from Puebla, and have brought some fine eating with them, notably mole poblano.

Legend has it that mole poblano (a thick, dark blend of chili and dark bitter chocolate), a culinary contribution from Puebla, was invented by nuns trying to create a dish worthy of a visiting dignitary. Holy mole! Pueblan cooking also favors vegetables stuffed with meat, nuts, and raisins, and covered with creamy sauces.

Veracruz, another Mexican culinary high spot famous for seafood and ceviche is the home town of many of Queens' Mexicans. Any fish dish a la Veracruzana means it'll be topped with a sauce of tomatoes, olives, capers, and chilies.

DESSERTS

Mexicans like their sweets as much as any culture. Flan places high on the list, as does pastel des tres leches (three-milk cake), an ultra-moist cake saturated with a syrup of sweetened condensed milk,

evaporated milk, and heavy cream.

Some of the wildest Mexican desserts are associated with the holiday Dia de Los Muertos (Day of the Dead). This holiday of remembrance of lost loved ones is celebrated on November 1 with breads, cakes, and sweets fashioned to look like skulls or skeletons. Toward the end of October, look for muertitos (little dead ones), loaves of sugar-sprinkled bread resembling infants with arms crossed over their chest.

BEVERAGES

Tequila, Mexico's most famous spirit, is made from the agave, a member of the lily family (and not a cactus as many people think). A mild, fermented drink made from agave was enjoyed by the Aztecs for centuries. When the Spanish arrived, they applied their knowledge of distillation to this indigenous drink, and tequila was born.

Everyone has heard of the margarita, the most famous tequila-based drink. Served in a salt-rimmed glass, and served frozen (or not), it tends to appeal more to tourists. Mexicans are as apt to drink a brandy and Coke.

Beer and Mexican food go together like cookies and milk.

Germans founded the first breweries in Mexico and introduced beer drinking to the culture. There are two main breweries in Mexico: Grupo Modelo, which produces Corona, Negra Modelo, Modelo Especial, and Victoria; and Cuauhtemoc Moctezuma, whose brews include Sol, Tecate, XX, Bohemia, and Noche Buena.

When it comes to nonalcoholic beverages, Mexicans make a really first-rate hot chocolate from solid blocks of drinking chocolate melted in warmed milk and frothed with a molinillo, a wooden gadget designed for that purpose. Atole is a warm, almost porridge-like drink made thick with masa (corn flour). The chocolate version is known as champurrado; other versions are flavored with fruits or nuts.

Mexicans grow and drink plenty of coffee. One of the most interesting ways they prepare it is in cafe de olla, which translates to "coffee from the pot." This much-loved syrupy-sweet coffee drink, prepared with cinnamon and cloves, can be made in 20 minutes, but can be simmered in the pot all day long.

Horchata is a refreshing cold drink made of rice, almonds, cinnamon (canella), lime zest, and sugar. This drink is rumored to be a cure for a hangover and is frequently served at breakfast. Though the drink has a milky appearance, it's completely dairy-free. Agua de tamarindo (tamarind cooler) is a slightly sweet, tart beverage served throughout Mexico and Central America. It's the Mexican answer to lemonade.

MEXICAN RESTAURANTS

Viko's Cafe

41-07 National St., Corona, 718-651-4595
Subway: No. 7 to 103rd St.-Corona Plaza
This is a darling little place operated by Viko Ortega, a Pueblan native. It's tucked away and easy to miss, but well worth the effort of finding it. The restaurant serves deliciously authentic Mexican breakfast, lunch, and dinner. Viko also operates La Flor (53-02 Roosevelt Ave., Woodside, 718-426-8023), which provides the desserts for Viko's Cafe but is more eclectic than Mexican.

Taqueria Coatzingo

76-05 Roosevelt Ave., Jackson Heights
718-424-1977

Subway: E or F to Roosevelt Ave., Jackson Heights, or No. 7 to 74th St.

Tops for tortas and cemitas.

El Jarro Cafe
45-02 48th Ave., Woodside
718-392-2161
Subway: No. 7 to 46th St.
Tiny and unpretentious, the Poblano en Nogales, a stuffed poblano chili with pork, dried fruit, and nuts, served in a lush walnut-pomegranate cream sauce served here is heaven.

Tierras Mexicanas
31-01 36th Ave., Astoria
718-777-6603
Subway: N or W to 36th Ave.
Great food in an upscale ambiance.

Fiesta Mexicana
75-02 Roosevelt Ave., Jackson Heights
718-505-9090
Subway: No. 7 to 46th St.
Easy to get to (right near the subway). Hard to resist.

Original Mexican Food (formerly called Hidalgo Mexican Food Products)
30-11 29th St., Astoria,
718-274-6936
Subway: N to 30th Ave.

This is a Mexican grocery store with a counter serving outstanding Mexican food. Try the tamales, although it's hard to miss with whatever you choose.

Mexican Torta

INGREDIENTS

1 cup mayonnaise

2 canned chipotle chilies in adobo sauce

4 Mexican-style soft rolls (bolillo or telera), split in half

1 pound cooked chicken, ham, or roast pork, thinly sliced

4 medium tomatoes, thinly sliced

1 Hass avocado, peeled, seeded, and cut into 16 thin slices

8 slices Oaxaca cheese (or jack)

DIRECTIONS

Preheat oven to 350 degrees Fahrenheit. Place the mayonnaise and chipotle chilies in a food processor and blend until smooth. Generously spread the cut sides of the rolls with the chipotle mayonnaise. Cover the bottom half of each roll with sliced meat. Top each portion of meat with slices of tomato and avocado. Cover with 2 slices of cheese. Place assembled open-faced sandwiches on a cookie sheet or pan and bake until cheese is melted, about 8 minutes. Cover the sandwiches, slice in half, and serve immediately.

SERVES 4.

Sopa de Tortilla *(Tortilla soup)*

INGREDIENTS

3 tablespoons olive oil

4 corn tortillas, torn into spoon-sized pieces

5 garlic cloves, minced

1 large onion, puréed

3 large, ripe tomatoes, peeled and puréed

1/4 cup canned tomato purée

1/4 cup fresh lime juice

1 tablespoon chili powder

1 teaspoon ground cumin

1 tablespoon canned chipotle chilies in adobo sauce

1/2 cup fresh cilantro leaves, chopped

2 quarts homemade chicken stock with meat reserved (skin and bones removed), or an equal amount of canned chicken broth in which a boneless chicken breast has been boiled for 40 minutes and reserved

salt and pepper, to taste

garnishes: chunks of skinless boneless white chicken meat; 1 ripe Haas avocado, peeled, seeded, and chopped; Queso Ranchero—tortillas that have been cut into thin strips and fried until crisp like Chinese noodles

DIRECTIONS

Heat the olive oil in a large soup pot. Sauté the tortilla pieces with the garlic until tortillas soften. Add the puréed onion and tomato and bring to a boil. Add the tomato purée, lime juice, chili powder, cumin, chipotle chilies in adobo sauce, 1/2 of the cilantro, and the chicken stock. Bring to a boil again. Reduce heat, cover, and simmer for 30 minutes. Check seasonings, and add salt and pepper as desired. Garnish each serving with cooked chicken breast, avocado, queso ranchero, chopped cilantro, and crisp tortilla strips.

SERVES 4-6.

◉ EL SALVADOR

MEXICAN EATERIES FAR OUTSTRIP ANY
other Central American cuisine in terms of
number and visibility of establishments. This is
partly because Central Americans tend to migrate
between countries, and the offerings at Latino
restaurants are often more pan-Latino than from
strictly one community. But one other country
that has left its mark on the borough is El
Salvador.

The Salvadoran diet, like the diet in other Central American countries, relies on a couple of mainstays: rice and beans (casamiento), fried plantains, corn tortillas, tamales, fresh seafood, shrimp ceviche, chorizo, and grilled steak. El Salvador's main culinary contribution to the world is the pupusa. Salvadoran restaurants are sometimes called pupuserías. A pupusa is a rounded corn meal dough, usually stuffed with various fillings. Cheese, chicharrones (fried pork rinds), and refried beans are the most common. Typically, a pupusa is somewhat heavy and oily. The obligatory accompaniment is curtido, sliced cabbage marinated in vinegar—a Salvadoran coleslaw.

In their native land, Salvadorans have a fondness for armadillo stew, iguana soup, and iguana eggs served as a beach snack. Those specialties don't seem to have reached our shores.

Salvadoran beverages and dessert are pretty much the same as you would find in a Mexican establishment. The local beer is Regia Extra.

SALVADORAN RESTAURANTS

Rincon Salvadoreno
92-15 149th St., Jamaica
718-536-3220
Subway: F to Sutphin Blvd.
A lively and festive spot to sample Salvadoran.

La Nueva Izalco Salvadorean Restaurant
64-05 Roosevelt Ave., Woodside
718 533-8373
Subway: 61st St.-Woodside
Izalco is the name of a volcano in El Salvador.

◉ DOMINICAN REPUBLIC

THE CARIBBEAN CUISINES ARE LARGELY defined by who colonized each country. The Latino Caribbean cuisine most accessible in Queens is Dominican. There may be a lot more Puerto Ricans in Queens than Dominicans, but they don't seem to have gone into the restaurant business.

Dominican cuisine (comida criolla) is a fusion of the influences of Taino Indians, Spanish people, and African slaves. Although the Dominican Republic is a Caribbean country, many of its favorite dishes have a lot in common with Colombia. The national dish is sancocho, also a Colombian specialty. Other gastric convergences include snacking on chicarrones (fried pork skin) and tostones (fried plantains).

BREAKFAST

Yaniqueques (johnnycakes, or fried, crunchy tortillas) and mangú (a purée made of boiled plantains, also eaten as a snack) make up the favorite Dominican breakfast.

SNACKS AND APPETIZERS

The Dominican contributions to happy snacking include mofongo (balls of mashed plantains that have been salted and roasted), yucca balls (the same, only made from yucca), pastelitos (meat- or cheese-filled pastry turnovers), and quipes (ground beef encased in cracked wheat). For something more substantial, chimichurris (not to be confused with the

Argentinean sauce) are delicious pork sandwiches made from meat cooked on a spit.

MAIN DISHES

In the Dominican Republic, sancocho is a meat and vegetable stew that might contain anything from pork and seafood to sweet potatoes and cassava. Sancocho prieto is a hearty black stew made with seven different kinds of meats.

Sancocho may be the national dish, but the most emblematic offering (literally) is known as La Bandera, "The Flag," because it includes the colors of the Dominican flag: white rice, red beans, stewed meats, salad, and tostones (fried green plantains). Chicken is the most popular meat, and no Dominican eatery would create a menu without a good arroz con pollo (chicken mixed with rice).

Rice is the staple food served with everything. Locrio is the Dominican rice dish that locals believe was the answer to the Spanish question "Can someone here make me some paella?" Not having the traditional ingredients, substitutions were made, like using annatto instead of saffron. Today ingredients vary, depending on what's at hand.

DESSERTS

Since the Dominican Republic is a sugar-producing country, its cuisine contains a variety of sweets and desserts. Flan is the top of the pops when it comes to dessert, with coconut flan the most popular of numerous varieties. Other famous specialties are dulce de coco (coconut sweet), dulce de leche, and dulce de batata (sweet potato candy).

DOMINICAN RESTAURANTS

Gran Rancho Jubilee
23-04 94th St., East Elmhurst
718-335-1700
Subway: N or W to Astoria Blvd., then M 60 Bus to 94th St.
The décor here offers a fun, over-the-top taste of the tropics. Lots of bamboo and thatch.

Amolex Restaurant
102-47 43rd Ave., Corona
718-779-5757
Subway: No. 7 to 103rd St. Station

Quisqueya Restaurant
97-03 Roosevelt Ave, Corona
718-478-0704
Subway: No. 7 to Junction Blvd.

⊙ JAMAICA

ONE OF THE PLUSES OF EXPLORING Jamaican restaurants is that Jamaicans speak English. Nonetheless, having an interpreter can come in handy. I struck gold when I chanced to meet Paulette Clarke, a Jamaican who lives in Queens and manufactures her own line of jerk sauces and seasonings under the "MsWhirls" brand name. No one could have been more authoritative or articulate in helping me navigate the intricacies of Jamaican cuisine.

Jamaican food is a vibrant fusion of culinary traditions. It contains elements from the original Arawak and Carib indigenous tribes, West African ingredients introduced by the slaves, and South and East Asian culinary influences brought by laborers from India and China after slavery was abolished, tempered by the bland, stodgy dining habits of the British colonial influence.

Food historians credit the Caribs with introducing the spicing of food with chili peppers. The Arawaks are believed to have originated barbecue by making grills with native green sticks called barbacoa, a term that later morphed into the familiar "barbecue." Arawak crops included taro root, corn, yams, cassava, and

IRISH MOSS DRINK, MADE FROM SEAWEED, CAN BE PREPARED FRESH, OR FOUND IN CANS IN CARIBBEAN MARKETS

peanuts. Guava and pineapple, as well as black-eyed peas and lima beans, grew wild on the islands. The West African slaves brought okra, pigeon peas, plantains, callaloo, eddo (taro or coco), and ackee. Breadfruit was introduced from Fiji by Captain William Bligh of *Mutiny on the Bounty* fame.

Primary ingredients of the Jamaican diet are fish, chicken, vegetables, exotic fruit, and pepper-based spices, either mild or incendiary. Jamaican vegetables include cho-cho (also called christophine or chayote), a pulpy, squash-like vegetable reputed to lower blood pressure. Callaloo (also

spelled calalou) is a Jamaican spinach, and the principal ingredient of the island's famous pepper pot soup. Jamaicans use the terms peas and beans interchangeably, and the popular side dish of rice and peas (never peas and rice,) usually made from gungo beans (pigeon peas), is served in most restaurants. Okra, potatoes, yams, and cassava are also common. Cassava was grown by the Arawaks and used to make laundry starch. Originally, the leftovers from starch making were pounded and prepared to make another national favorite, bammy, a heavy but tasty starch cake served as a side dish or at breakfast. Fried plantain, a member of the banana family popular throughout the Caribbean and South America, is also often eaten as a side dish.

BREAKFAST

Ackee is the national dish of Jamaica, and ackee with saltfish (salted dried cod) is the national breakfast dish. It was introduced from west Africa in the 18th century, and its name derives from the West African akye fufo. The plant was later named blighia sapida in honor of Captain Bligh, who took samples to Kew in 1793.

This fruit turns red when mature and splits open with continued exposure to the sun. Consumption of unripe fruit can cause acute digestive problems, but since all of what's served in Queens is canned, there's nothing to worry about on that score.

Ackee and saltfish is a must-try if you're within striking distance of a Jamaican restaurant at breakfast. In appearance, it resembles scrambled eggs, especially if the cooking fat used is a few slices of bacon. Presoaked boiled saltfish is added to the scramble along with onions and peppers to make a breakfast dish not so radically different from a typical American breakfast. Try it with bammy that's been soaked in milk and fried. Callaloo is often steamed with saltfish and served for breakfast.

LUNCH

The patty is to Jamaicans what a hot dog is to Americans. Jamaican patties are perfect as a light lunch, snack, or street food. Culinary descendants of the Cornish pasty, they are a pastry-encased serving of highly seasoned (in some cases incendiary) minced beef, chicken, or vegetables, sometimes fried, sometimes baked. Jamaican also eat patties tucked in coco bread, a large soft roll. Pastry inside a roll may sound like gilding the lily, but if you're not low-carbing it, it's not bad. Another light lunch on the run is bun and cheese. The bun, in this case, is actually a slice of a ginger-spiced quick bread. The cheese is a Jamaican cheese that comes in a can and tastes something like Velveeta. Bun and cheese is a snack associated with Easter.

For a more substantial lunch, look for cowpea stew with dumplings. This is actually a stew of beef with beans (Jamaicans call red kidney beans "peas"). On the side, try some boiled green bananas. Stew peas (red kidney beans) with a pig's tail, or some

YUCCA AND OTHER CARIBBEAN PRODUCE

beef, is another possibility, especially with runners—elongated cassava dumplings. Jamaicans would probably eat some bits of cut-up Scotch bonnet peppers on the side with either of these dishes, never passing up the opportunity to add to the intensity of the heat.

DINNER

Jerked meats are Jamaica's most widely known and most popular food preparation. Pork, chicken, or fish is marinated in a fiery mixture of spices, including Scotch bonnet (a pepper that makes a jalapeño wimpy by comparison), pimento or allspice, nutmeg, and thyme. It's all served up with even more hot sauce, rice, and peas, and the wonderful festival bread. Jerked meats are one of the ultimate Jamaican dishes, dating back to the island's earliest days. The practice of cooking the meat over the flame was started by the Arawak Indians, and the seasonings were later perfected by the Maroons (runaway slaves and their descendants). When ordering in a Jamaican restaurant, make sure you load up on the ethnic sides for the truly authentic experience. Spicy curried goat is another big Jamaican favorite, and almost a requirement for a big celebration.

GOOD LUCK MONEY IN JAMAICAN RESTAURANT FROM U.S., JAMAICA, AND (COURTESY OF SOME GIS) IRAQ!

Sundays are when Jamaicans' British colonial roots are exposed. A proper Sunday dinner (and Sunday dinners are a big deal to Brits) in Jamaica would include either roast beef, which more closely resembles our pot roast, cooked in a Dutch oven nicknamed a "Dutchie," or else stewed chicken. Don't forget the rice and peas. Carrot juice is the preferred beverage on Sundays, made from carrot juice, condensed milk, and beetroot.

DESSERT

Jamaican desserts are another culinary tradition that betrays the country's colonial heritage. Jamaican fruitcake, almost black in color, is de rigueur at Christmas and weddings. It's made from dried fruit (raisins, currants, etc.) that's been ground and macerated for up to a year in rum and port, then mixed with a cake batter and baked or steamed like plum pudding. Sweet potato pudding is also a favorite. It's made from either yam or coco (eddo), combined with coconut milk, raisins, and sugar. Jamaican ice cream comes in a variety of tropical flavors like grape nut (also called great nut), rum raisin, and soursop. Tamarind candy is a popular treat, having both a sweet and tart flavor.

BEVERAGES

Columbus introduced sugarcane in Jamaica in 1493. It was later discovered that rum could be made from fermented cane juice. No more need be said. Jamaican liqueurs come in tropical flavors like soursop, papaw, and, of course, coffee, as in Tia Maria. Red Stripe Beer is the local brew, and Dragon Stout is another popular reflection of Brit sensibilities. Jamaicans will drink Dragon Stout on Sundays mixed with condensed milk.

Jamaican soft drinks come in a vast array of intriguing tropical flavors. The term tea is used interchangeably for various hot and cold drinks. Irish moss drink, which looks and sounds revolting but is actually quite tasty, is made from Irish moss (a kind of seaweed) and condensed milk. It tastes like a smoothie of indeterminate flavor, and can be had either freshly made or bottled.

Jamaican ginger beer is bracing—not at all like wimpy American ginger ale. Ting is a flavorful sweet/tart carbonated grapefruit soda. At Christmas, a drink made from sorrel berries steeped with ginger and brown sugar is popular.

JAMAICAN AND WEST INDIAN RESTAURANTS

The Door
163-07 Baisley Blvd., Jamaica
718-525-1083
Subway: E, J, Z to Jamaica Center/Parsons, then Q 111 bus to Baisley Blvd.
The restaurant dishes up Jamaican food in fairly elegant surroundings while keeping its prices modest. It serves a range of traditional Jamaican dishes, and also some American fare. The restaurant tones down the traditional spiciness of the food to appeal to a broader range of palates, but will make your food extra spicy on request. Breakfast, lunch, dinner, and take-out, seven days a week.

Country Style
215-09 Jamaica Ave., Queens Village
718-468-3500
Subway: F to 179th St., then Q 36 bus to 215th St.
For home-style Jamaican food, this place has it all. Truly authentic. Serving breakfast, lunch, and dinner to eat in or take out.

Jean's Restaurant
188-36 Linden Blvd., St. Albans
718-525-3069

Subway: E, F, or J to Jamaican Center, then Q 04 to Linden Blvd. and 188th St.

Jean's is a popular spot offering West Indian and American food. Jamaican wines and rum punch are also available, along with Jamaican ice cream and Jamaican-style milkshakes with Irish moss and carrot juice.

GLOSSARY OF JAMAICAN FOOD TERMS

Ackee: Fruit that, after cooking, resembles scrambled eggs; usually served with saltfish (cod)

Bammy: Flat cassava cake

Boiled green banana: Unripe banana, boiled and salted

Bulla: A sweet cake or cookie

Bun: A spicy bread eaten with cheese, especially at Easter

Cow foot stew: Cow hooves and beans

Cut cake: A sweet cake made with diced coconut and ginger

Duckanoo: The recipe for duckanoo was brought from Africa; a dessert made with cornmeal, coconut, spices, and brown sugar, all of which are tied up in a banana leaf (hence its other names, Blue Drawers and Tie-A-Leaf) and slowly cooked in boiling water

Escovitch: A style of cooking using vinegar, onions, and spices, brought to Jamaica from Spain. In Jamaican grocery stores you can also find bottled escovitch sauce to make the preparation easier

Escovitch fish: A contribution from the Spanish Jews who lived on the island nearly 500 years ago; fried fish marinated with vinegar

Festival: A deep-fried cornmeal fritter frequently served with jerk, similar to a hush puppy

Gizzada: A coconut tart

Grater cake: A confection made from grated coconut and sugar; usually pink and white

Gungo: Pigeon peas

Hard dough or hard dough bread: A staple brought to Jamaica by the Chinese

Irish moss: Gelatinous extract of seaweed, which can be mixed with milk, nutmeg, or rum and used as a drink or jelly; said to be an aphrodisiac

Ital food (pronounced (eye-tal): The food of the Rastafarians, a vegetarian cuisine that does not use salt

Janga: Small crayfish

Jerk: Slow-roasted meat prepared with a mixture of spices, not sparing the heat

Johnnycake: Sometimes called journey cakes (since you could carry them along on your journey); actually fried or baked breads; a favorite accompaniment to saltfish

Mannish water: A spicy soup (reportedly an aphrodisiac, along with many other Jamaican specialties); sometimes called power water; made from goats' heads (some cooks include tripe and feet as well), garlic, scallions, cho-cho, green bananas, Scotch bonnet peppers, and spinners; white rum is optional

Matrimony: A Christmas dessert of orange segments with crushed purple star apples in cream

Mauby: A strong drink made from the eponymous tree; tastes like muscular sarsaparilla

Pepper pot soup: A peppery soup of callaloo (which gives this island favorite its green color), and may include pig tails or salt pork (sometimes salt beef), coconut milk, okra, and plenty of spices

Pone: Pudding

Pumpkin soup: Caribbean pumpkins are not large and sweet like their American counterparts, but small and a favorite soup ingredient

Red pea soup: A soup made from kidney beans, salted pig tails, beef, and vegetables

Rice and peas: A popular side dish; the peas can be gunga beans or kidney beans

Rundown: This entrée is pickled fish cooked in a seasoned coconut milk until the fish falls apart or literally "runs down"

Salomon Gundy: Pickled, spiced herring

Saltfish: Salted cod

Sorrel: Flowering plant from which sweet jams, candies, drinks, and wine are made, often served during the Christmas holidays

Spinners Dumplings: found in soups and stews; they take their name from their thin, twisted shape

Stew peas: Made with either red peas or gungo peas, this soup also includes pork and coconut milk

Tie-a-Leaf: See duckanoo (above)

Turned cornmeal: Cooked cornmeal in seasoned coconut milk, with meat and/or vegetables

Ackee and Saltfish

INGREDIENTS

1/2 pound saltfish

1 can ackees

1 tablespoon oil or 4 slices of bacon

1 medium onion, chopped

black pepper to taste

DIRECTIONS

Soak saltfish in cold water overnight. Pour off water, add fresh water, and cook until tender or sufficient salt has been removed. Remove bones and flake saltfish. Meanwhile, allow ackees to drain. In a frying pan, sauté bacon (if used) or heat oil. Add onion and cook until transparent. Add flaked saltfish, ackees, and black pepper. Scramble together. Serve immediately.

SERVES 4.

Jamaican-Style Jerk Chicken

INGREDIENTS

2-3 pounds chicken pieces, bone in

5-6 tablespoons MsWhirls Authentic Jamaican-Style Jerk Seasoning

2 tablespoons shortening (butter, margarine, or oil)

pinch of salt

1/2 cup water

DIRECTIONS

Clean and cut chicken into medium-size pieces. Rub jerk seasoning on all chicken surfaces. Set aside for 45 minutes or more. Heat butter, margarine, or oil in a deep skillet. Add chicken pieces, salt, and water. Cover tightly and let simmer until chicken is cooked. Serve with rice and peas or white rice.

SERVES 5-6.

Contributed by Paulette U. Clarke, MsWhirls Enterprises Inc., manufacturers of MsWhirls Authentic Jamaican Style Jerk Seasoning. For information or to order, visit www.mswhirls.com, call 718-468-9540, or e-mail sales@mswhirls.com.

◉ GUYANA

IN AND AROUND RICHMOND HILL, there's a growing Indo-Caribbean population, mostly from Guyana. Along Liberty Avenue, store after store sells goods that appear to cater to East Indians. In actual fact, they are aimed at clientele that claims Indian ancestry but that long ago settled in Guyana.

Guyana claims six major races: Afro-Guyanese, Amerindians, East Indians, Portuguese, Chinese, whites, and a mixed race. The Chinese seem to have exerted the most powerful culinary influence. Menus from Queens's Guyanese restaurants read more like a Chinese menu with some peculiar combinations than a cohesive cuisine. Any given menu will include lengthy lists of offerings from such categories as "fried rice," "lo mein," "chow mein," various meat and seafood dishes listed under the type of meat, and "West Indian Dishes," mainly curries.

How does Jerk Chicken Chow Mein sound? Maybe Jerk Pork Lo Mein or Roast Lamb Fried Rice appeals.

Like the rest of us, the Guyanese are big snackers. Most of their snack foods are deep-fried. Egg balls, seemingly the tropical cousin of Scotch eggs (Britain's sausage-encased deep-fried hard-boiled eggs), are hard-boiled eggs encased in cassava and deep-fried. Dhalpouri (there are many different spellings), a treat with East Indian roots, is a round puffy roti filled with lentil puree. Phoulorie are deep-fried balls of garlicky

BANANA FLOWERS ARE USED AS WRAPPINGS FOR VARIOUS STUFFINGS IN MANY TROPICAL CULTURES INCLUDING LATINO AND SOUTHEAST ASIAN

reconstituted chick-pea flour.

The Chinese dishes taste more or less like Americanized Chinese food (Chinese people don't eat chow mein), but with a kick. Even plain fried rice delivers an after burn.

Guyanese curries pack a wallop and are closer to Jamaica curries than to East Indian curries, but they sort of meet each other halfway. They are closer to south Indian curries than to north, but don't use coconut milk.

The favorite vegetable is bora (long bean), often mixed with cabbage. The usual hot pepper is the wirri-wirri, a small berrylike pepper with a characteristic flavor and plenty of heat (though it can't compete with the Scotch bonnet).

Some of Queens's Guyanese restaurants have bakeries on the premises. Look for items like tennis rolls (round rolls resembling tennis balls), butter flap (a tennis ball with butter), cheese roll (a slightly spicy roll), black bean (Chinese-inspired), and plait, a thick, braid-shaped egg loaf.

DESSERTS

Desserts in Guyana run along the same lines as in Jamaica. Look for an assortment of cakes and sweets featuring tropical ingredients. Expect to find a pine tart (pineapple-filled triangular pastry) and coconut cake. Ice cream in tropical flavors, especially coconut, is a typical Guyanese dessert.

BEVERAGES

The Guyanese drink Banks beer, local rum, brandy, whisky, and delicious fruit punches. Many of the same exotic soft drinks seen in Jamaican restaurants turn up in Guyanese restaurants, including ginger beer, sea moss, and sorrel.

GUYANESE RESTAURANTS

Bamboo Garden
114-09 Liberty Ave., Richmond Hill
718-843-0754
Subway: A to 111th St.

Full range of Guyanese Chinese and West Indian dishes with bakery. Great selection of sides.

The Nest
125-17 101st Ave., Richmond Hill
718-847-4035
Subway: A to Lefferts Blvd.
Nice ambience, but a long walk from the subway.

Sybil's Bakery
132-17 Liberty Ave., Richmond Hill
718-835 9235
Subway: A to Lefferts Blvd.
The oldest Guyanese restaurant in the area. Owner Sybil Kerrutt passed away recently, but her restaurant lives on.

Kaieteur Restaurant and Sports Bar
87-12 Lefferts Blvd., Richmond Hill
718-850-0707
Subway: J or Z to 121st St.
Named for a waterfall in Guyana. Serves Chinese and West Indian dishes.

Singh's Roti Shop #3
118-06 Liberty Ave., Richmond Hill
718-835-7255

Subway: A to Lefferts Blvd.
The Indo-Caribbean take on
Guyanese food. It offers mainly
wraps served in (what else?) rotis,
the Indian grilled, unleavened
flatbread. They come with a variety
of spicy fillings, and a vegetable
and starch on the side. Similar to
Indian snack food, but with a
detectable Caribbean accent.

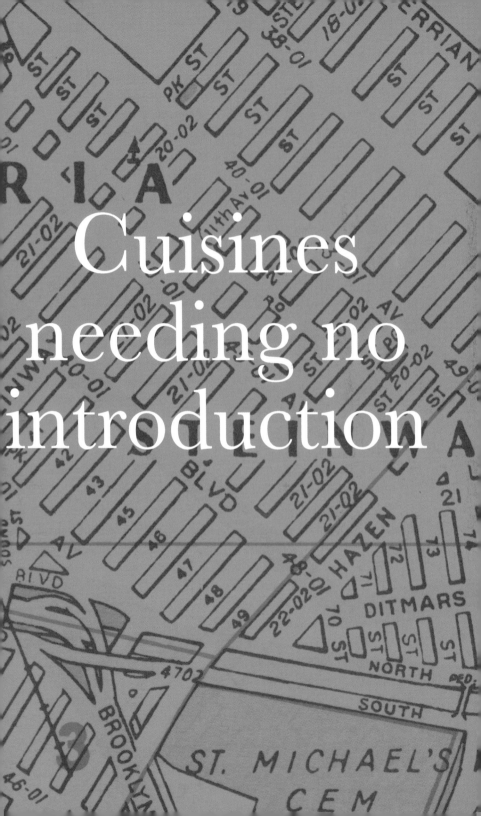

Cuisines
needing no
introduction

⊙ EVERY FOOD IS AN ETHNIC FOOD TO SOMEONE ELSE.

I AM REMINDED OF THE TIME WHEN I observed a group of Japanese tourists in an American buffet-style restaurant in Hawaii get giggly over the prospect of eating with a knife and fork.

Over the years, just as immigrant groups have assimilated, America has embraced a broad range of cuisines as their own. There is a wealth of irresistible Queens eateries where you should be able to navigate the menu without coaching. Here is a roundup of some of the best.

ITALIAN

An entire directory could be written about Queens's Italian eateries, but I have winnowed the list to some of my personal favorites.

Trattoria L'incontro
21-76 31st St., Astoria
718-721-3532
Subway: N, W to Astoria/Ditmars Blvd.
Serious eaters who appreciate fine traditional and updated Italian fare and don't mind bustling, sometimes hectic surroundings will find what they crave.

Sapori d'Ischia
55-15 37th Ave., between 55th and 56th streets, Woodside
718-446-1500
Subway: G, R to Northern Blvd.
An Italian-foods warehouse and retail store by day, and a fun Italian

THE BEST VIEWS OF THE INNER BOROUGH ARE FROM QUEENS. SOME OF LONG ISLAND'S EATERIES OFFER DINING ROOMS WITH GLORIOUS VIEWS OF MANHATTAN.

dining destination by night. Don't be put off by the gritty commercial neighborhood. Worth the trek.

Altadonna
249-30 Horace Harding Expwy., Little Neck
718-224-5474
Subway: F to 169th St., Q 30 Bus to 249th St.
Delicious homey Italian, with an emphasis on Sicilian specialties.

La Tavernetta
75-01 88th St. (between Cooper Ave. and Union Turnpike), Glendale

718-896-3538
No viable public transportation.
An inexpensive Italian gem tucked away in a Glendale backwater. Pasta to die for.

Piccola Venezia
42-01 28th Ave., Astoria
718-721-8470
Subway: G, R, V to Steinway St.; N, W to 30th Ave.
Excellent, lavish (if pricey) Italian fare.

Leo's Latticini
46 02 104th St., Flushing
718-898-6069

Subway: No. 7 to 103rd St.-Corona
Plaza
This family-run Italian deli makes
the best hero sandwiches you're
gonna find. A stone's throw from
Shea Stadium; you may find
yourself standing in line with one
of the Mets.

PIZZA
Nick's Pizza
108-26 Ascan Ave., Forest Hills
718-263-1126
Subway: E or F to 75th Ave.
Pizza lovers preferring a crispy thin
crust will find top-notch wood-fired
brick oven pizza made with first-
rate ingredients.

Dee's Brick Oven Pizza
107-23 Metropolitan Ave., Forest
Hills
718-793-7553
Subway: E or F to 71st
/Continental Ave., then Q 23 bus
to Metropolitan Ave.
New larger location should
accommodate the crowds that
milled around outside the former
location waiting for a table on
Saturday nights. Extensive selection
of designer pizza, pasta specialties,
and Mediterranean odds and ends.

FRENCH
Tournesol
50-12 Vernon Blvd., Long Island
City
718-472-4355
Subway: No. 7 to Vernon
Blvd.–Jackson Ave.
Tiny, delightful, sunflower-themed
French bistro.

Restaurant Seven One Eight
35-01 Ditmars Blvd., Astoria
718-204-5553
Subway: N, W to Astoria–Ditmars
Blvd.
A terrific French bistro with
Spanish influence. Offerings
include tapas and tarte flambée, a
sort of Alsatian pizza.

Le Sans Souci
44-09 Broadway at 44th St.,
Astoria
718-728-2733
Subway: R, V, G to 46th St.
You can easily imagine yourself in
Brittany here. A Francophile's
paradise.

IRISH
BREAKFAST
Shane's Bakery & Cafe
39-61 61st St., Woodside
718-424-9039
Subway: No. 7 to 61st St.
Soul-satisfying Irish breakfast and

light fare; fabulous scones.

SEAFOOD

London Lennie's
63-88 Woodhaven Boulevard.,
Rego Park
718-894-8084
Subway: G, R, V to 63rd Dr.–Rego
Park
An upscale Queens seafood
institution.

Elias Corner
24-02 31st St., Astoria
718-932-1510
Subway: N, W to Astoria Blvd.
Greek-style seafood. Whole grilled
fish is its forte. No menus.

GREEK

S'Agapo
34-21 34th Ave., Astoria
718-626-0303
Subway: G, R, V to Steinway St.;
N, W to Broadway
Quality Greek cuisine, especially
delectable dips and starters.

Philoxenia
26–18 23rd Ave., Astoria
718-626-9162
Subway: N, W to Ditmars Blvd.
Small and homey Greek eatery, like
your Greek grandma's.

Karyatis Restaurant
35-03 Broadway, Astoria
718-204-0666
Subway: N, W to Broadway
Nicely appointed, serving
dependable Greek fare.

Esperides Restaurant
37-01 30th Ave.
718-545-1494
Subway: R, V, G to Steinway St.
Outstanding Greek seafood, a little
on the pricey side for the nabe.

SUSHI

Sushi has become so ubiquitous at
supermarkets that it seems about as
foreign as spaghetti. Here are some
super spots to enjoy raw fish and
other related fare.

Mickey's Sushi
101-16 Queens Blvd. (between 67th
Dr. & 67th Rd.)
718-897-9898
Subway: R, V, G to 67th Ave.
Great, tiny, homey sushi place.

JJ'S Fusion Kitchen & Sushi Bar
37-05 31 Ave., Astoria
718-626-8888
Subway: N or W to 30th Ave.
Sushi and French fusion sushi from
a chef who studied at the French
Culinary Institute.

Sato Japanese Restaurant
98-12 Queens Blvd., Rego Park
718-897-1788
Subway: R, V, G to 67th Ave.
Say "konichi-wa" to the suit of bogu (the protective armor worn by practitioners of Kendo) that greets you up front. Traditional Japanese fare and sushi, and western-influenced flights of fancy from a Japanese chef who was raised and began his career in Paris.

SOUL FOOD/ BARBECUE

Mo's Southern BBQ
163-17 Archer Ave. (corner of Guy R. Brewer Blvd.), Jamaica
718-785-4000
Subway: E, J, Z to Jamaica Center-Parson/Archer
Some pretty darn good barbecue and soul food with transcendent sides.

ICE CREAM

Eddie's Sweet Shop
105-29 Metropolitan Ave., Forest Hills
718-520-8514
Subway: E or F to 71st /Continental Ave., then Q 23 bus to Metropolitan Ave.
Century-old soda fountain mostly untouched by time. Homemade ice cream and the best whipped cream and hot fudge you can find anywhere.

Lemon Ice King of Corona
52-02 108th St., Corona
718-699-5133
Subway: No. 7 to 103rd St., then Q 23 bus to 52nd Ave.
Legend has it that Frank Sinatra would send his driver to pick up

some of this divine Italian water ice. Offers an exhaustive list of flavors, all made with the real thing. If it's a fruit flavor, there are bits of the actual fruit.

NOT JUST FOR THE VIEW

Water's Edge Restaurant
44th Dr. at the East River, Long Island City
718-482-0033
Subway: E, V to 23rd St./Ely Ave.; 7 to 45th Rd./Court House Sq
There's no place in Manhattan that offers as good a view of Manhattan as this part of Queens. Soak it up in luxurious surroundings here. The restaurant a complimentary ferry from and to East 34th Street Pier. Try to time your visit for sunset.

Riverview
2-01 50th Ave., Long Island City
718-392-5000
Subway: No. 7 to Vernon Jackson Blvd.
Spectacular view and wonderful French-accented eclectic fare. Sleekly elegant décor.

SPANISH/TAPAS

El Boqueron
31-01 34th Ave., Astoria
718-956-0107
Subway: N, W to Broadway
Tops for tapas.

Mesón Asturias
40-12 83rd St. (between Baxter and Roosevelt aves.), Jackson Heights
718-446-9154
Subway: No. 7 to 82nd St.-Jackson Heights
The shrimp is garlic lovers' heaven. Flamenco on the weekends.

Pimenton
21-50 44th Dr. between 21st and 23rd Sts., Long Island City
718-707-0442
Subway: E, V to 23rd St.–Ely Ave.; G to Long Island City–Court Sq.; 7 to 45th Rd.–Court House Sq.
Tapas or paella in a charming town house or outdoor garden. Great eats if you hit it right, but the service and food can be unpredictably uneven.

La Vuelta
10-43 44th Dr., Long Island City
718-361-1858
Subway: E, V to 23rd St.–Ely Ave.; 7 to 45th Rd.–Court House Sq.
Spanish/Latino fare. Lots of art. Frequent special events and music.

JEWISH

Ben's Best
96-40 Queens Blvd., Rego Park
718- 897-1700
Subway: G, V, R to 63rd Dr.
Arguably the best Jewish deli in the
city. Pastrami from heaven. Slightly
grungy surroundings.

Knish Nosh
100-30 Queens Blvd., Rego Park
Subway: G, V, R to 67th Ave.
718-897-5554
"If you're only going to do one
thing, do it well," must be the
motto of this time-tested
establishment. The name says it all.

BAGELS

Utopia Bagels
19-09 Utopia Pkwy., Whitestone
718-352-2586
Closest to the hand-rolled bagels of
bygone times.

Hot Bialys
116-63 Queens Blvd. (at 78th Ave.)
Forest Hills
718-544-0900
Subway: E or F to Union Turnpike
Deceptively named, this bagel
emporium is owned and run by
Thais.

GERMAN

Zum Stammtisch
69-46 Myrtle Ave., Glendale
718-386-3014
Subway: M or L to Wycoff/Myrtle
Avenue, then Q 55 Bus to 69th St.
Good sauerbraten and other
German fare.

BEER GARDEN

Bohemian Hall and Beer Garden
29-19 24th Ave., Astoria
718-274-4925
Subway: N, W to Astoria Blvd.
The last beer garden in NYC
began its life as a Czech fraternal
association. Drink beer outdoors on
balmy summer nights with Czech
snacks and sometimes music.

EASTERN EUROPEAN

Note: Queens's Eastern European
spots sometimes give off clannish
ethnic vibes. Don't be put off. Once
you settle in, you'll be treated well.

Djerdan
34-04A 31st Ave., Astoria
718-721-2694
Subway: N, W to Broadway
Bosnian grilled meats and boureks
(meat-, cheese-, and spinach- filled
pastries) in a homey setting.

Cevabdzinica Sarajevo
37-18 34th Ave. (38th St.), Astoria
718-752-9528
Subway: G, R, V to Steinway St.
Bosnian-style sausages, grilled
meats, and boureks.

Cina
45-17 28th Ave., Astoria
718-956-0372
Subway: R, V, G to 46th St.
Hearty Romanian fare in a
charming setting.

ECLECTIC
La Flor
53-02 Roosevelt Ave., Woodside
718-426-8023
Subway: No.7 to 52nd St.
Bakery and restaurant decorated
with flair and pique assiette
mosaics, serving an assortment of
Mexican and continental specialties
and outstanding baked goods.
Super breakfasts.

Angie's Kitchen
41-46 54th St., Woodside
718-651-2277
Subway: No. 7 to 52nd St.
Long on charm and imagination.
Brunch is served here every day.

Index

ALPHABETICAL LISTING OF RESTAURANTS

NAME	CUISINE	PAGE

NAME	CUISINE	PAGE

RESTAURANTS BY CUISINE

RESTAURANTS BY NEIGHBORHOOD

NAME   CUISINE   PAGE

RECIPES

RECIPES BY FOOD TYPE